D061974L

talking about
homosexuality

a congregational resource

holy conversations

A study tool for theological reflection around debates in the church that considers scripture, tradition, reason, and experience.

talking about
homosexuality

a congregational resource

Karen P. Oliveto, Kelly D. Turney,
and Traci C. West

THE
PILGRIM
PRESS
Cleveland

The Pilgrim Press
700 Prospect Avenue
Cleveland, Ohio 44115-1100
pilgrimpress.com

10 09 08 07 06 05   5 4 3 2 1

Library of Congress Cataloging-in-Publication Data
Oliveto, Karen P., 1958-
    Talking about homosexuality : a congregational resource / Karen P. Oliveto,
Kelly D. Turney, and Traci C. West.
      p. cm.
    Includes bibliographical references.
    ISBN 0-8298-1613-5 (pbk. : alk. paper)
    1. Homosexuality – Religious aspects – Christianity.   I. Turney, Kelly, 1965-
II. West, Traci C., 1959-   III. Title.   IV. Series.

BR115.H6O55 2005
261.8'35766 – dc22
                                              2005045819

Contents

Preface

Our passion for this work is deeply rooted in the three distinctive backgrounds each of us brings to it. As you will find in your own discussion groups, it is from our own, different experiences that we begin the shared conversation of this book, speaking first tentatively, then more boldly.

Despite many silly moments and much joking about sex, we did not always find the conversation among ourselves easy or encouraging. There are still times when the chasms between us seem impossible to bridge. Yet, we began the conversation nonetheless, with a commitment to take risks with one another, to uncover some of the very different messages we received growing up about sexuality and our bodies, about manners, about what was "acceptable" to say aloud, and about trusting others. And so we began....

One of us will never forget how, "when I was growing up, I would often awake to find new people in the house. During the night, foreign exchange students, family members passing through, friends of a friend had found their way to our home. They were always welcome. Folks of diverse sexual orientations, national and ethnic backgrounds, and with even greater diversity of opinions would come, and leave, intimately sharing, however briefly, the bathroom, the floor space in the living room, and my life with my immediate family. Some stayed only for a night or two; others became part of the family. Perhaps it is these early childhood experiences of providing hospitality to the stranger that have led me to want to discuss what it means to be hospitable people of God and to generate more places of hospitality."

One of us will never forget "the arguments on the playground with my white classmates. While growing up, I was one of very few

black students in a small, mostly white, private school. During re-
cess, I remember asking my friends lots of questions about racism,
like: why didn't they care about the raging conflicts on the news
about school busing for racial integration? Why didn't they recognize the inequality in their mom calling the woman of color who
did their housecleaning by her first name, while the housecleaner
called their mom by her last name? And, I angrily asked one friend
why she thought that I should 'just let it go' when a boy in our
class called me 'nigger.' Perhaps it is these childhood experiences
of confronting harmful social divisions in everyday relationships
that now lead me to consider how we can commit ourselves to
confronting harmful social divisions as a people of God."

One of us will never forget "the way my relatives valued stories.
Told and retold in the homestead of my great-grandparents, there
were stories of overcoming obstacles, of embarrassing moments,
of glory relived, told with some reverence and punctuated with
humor. But into this sheltered life also came stories from outside
my family — stories of alienation, scarcity, and oppression. I remember being shocked that such worlds could exist, that others'
stories were not equally valued or told. I began to realize how risky
it was for people to share their closeted experiences and thus how
important it was to receive these precious seldom-told stories. Perhaps it is this experience of opening myself to another's story —
no matter how different — that leads me to proclaim the power
of listening to each other's lives as people of God."

Motivated by such experiences, we are convinced of the need
to create a welcoming space in the church for authentic sharing
among strangers. There has to be a way to confront the harmful
divisions that exclusions and shaming based upon sexual orientation and sex/gender identity have caused. But it cannot happen
without strategies that empower us to take the risks of building
bridges between people, bridges that allow intimate sharing of our
life stories and Christian faith journeys. As relative strangers learning to risk authentic conversation, we three have been fortunate
that so many have chosen to offer their stories and ideas for this
book, sharing their grief or pain or fear about the church.

We recognize there's no shortage of ideology and debate about sexuality and Christian faith. There has been a flurry of national church resolutions, study documents, debates, networking meetings, votes on the exclusion/inclusion of gays and lesbians from ordination and the episcopacy, as well as on the celebration of holy union and marriage ceremonies for same-sex couples. There are rapidly growing, new Protestant denominations and independent local churches whose founding principles boldly declare God's love and acceptance of gays, lesbians, bisexuals, and transgender persons. At the same time there are several national coalitions in the United States working together across Protestant denominational lines to systematically cleanse mainline churches of their openness to what is seen by them as "the sin of homosexuality."

In many of the conversations about homosexuality and Christianity, there is an "us" versus "them" mentality, which encourages people to retreat into a defense of their own position and claim the higher moral ground. Theology, Christian tradition, and the Bible are either wielded as weapons to bludgeon those "on the other side" or treated dismissively as tainted with too much pain and prejudice.

But we invite you to do a new thing. We invite you to enter into a "holy conversation" that allows you to reflect on the specifics of your faith in God along with your understanding of sexuality. We invite you to enter into a holy conversation based upon your own reflections on sexuality and your Christian faith. Out of this faith context we invite you to consider what is right for our lives together in the church and the broader society as lesbians, gays, bisexuals, transgender persons, and heterosexuals. As you enter into this holy conversation we also invite you to consider how your racial and cultural assumptions contribute to it.

Who is inviting you to take up such a personal and challenging task? We are African American and European American clergy. We have served in academic, campus, and pastoral ministries. We have been pastors in small and large churches in rural, suburban, and urban settings, located in north Texas, New York, New England, California, and Georgia. Each of us brings a sexual orientation distinctly different from the other two. We bring New England, West Coast, and southern perspectives. We are United Methodists active in national ecumenical movements who have worked with our sisters and brothers in Presbyterian, United Church of Christ, Disciples of Christ, United Methodist, Episcopalian, Baptist, Metropolitan Community Church, and African Methodist Episcopal churches. We have worked on issues of sexuality, violence against women, racism, poverty, AIDS, affirmative action, addiction, and prisoner rights. We have higher education degrees from schools in California, Connecticut, Tennessee, New York, and New Jersey. Two of us have Ph.D.s, and all of us have masters of divinity degrees.

There is so much more to be done than we can accomplish in this book. There are so many more stories to be heard about sexuality and faith than we have included. More focused attention should be given to crucial issues that intersect with the ones raised here. One such issue is gaining a better understanding of the varied expressions of bisexuality and of transgender identity and how they are part of expressions of Christian theology. A second is how one's socioeconomic class background and present economic circumstances impact conversations about sexuality and Christian faith. Though this book is only a beginning, we trust it will get you started on those conversations.

So we invite you to take a risk. Share in this holy conversation about faith and sexuality, for we believe that being in community with one another and discussing our views and stories of faithful sexuality enriches our lives. We believe that such conversations taking place in many, many local churches and communities will enrich the body of Christ. We believe that this dialogue does not have to be only contentious, divisive, and wounding but that such a conversation can indeed be sacred. It can draw us ever closer to the Holy One and to the holy in each of us.

Acknowledgments

This book would not have been possible without the hard work, vision, and witness of lesbians, gay men, transgender persons, bisexuals, and straight allies, both in the church and beyond it, who have committed themselves to full inclusion and equal rights in church and society for all God's children across all sex/gender identities and racial ethnic identities. Without their dedication, often in the face of hostility and hatred, the holy conversations we are seeking would not be possible.

We are particularly grateful to Marilyn Alexander for her vision and persistence in initially bringing us together to do this work. We are thankful for the *welcoming church movement* that has provided hope to LGBT people and their allies and continues to work for change in a church that wants none. The Reconciling Ministries Network in the United Methodist Church has been consistently supportive of this project.

We are grateful to those who share their stories in these pages as well as for the many LGBT folks who persist in believing that the church must include them and that it is an institution worthy of their insistence that it proclaim the inclusive message of the gospel.

As with any collaboration that links its participants across time zones and miles, there are a great many unsung helpers who send and receive faxes, troubleshoot technology problems, transport us to and from airports, arrange conference calls, and provide for our needs when we actually meet face to face. We are especially grateful to Uncle Howie Spence for his generous hospitality and care as we met in Nova Scotia, and to Teresa Gogan who tracked down our lost luggage so that the work could continue unabated, as well as to the Cumberland County Library System in Canada, particularly the Amherst and Springhill, Nova Scotia, branches.

We are grateful to our families, colleagues, friends, and employers who have been patient, indulgent, and supportive, including: Bethany United Methodist Church in San Francisco, California; Drew University in Madison, New Jersey; Trinity United Methodist Church in Springfield, Massachusetts; Robin Ridenour, Linda Campbell, Lori Stacy, Jane Ellen Nickell, Barbara Huber, Monica Ardolino, Mark Goad, Ed Farrell-Starbuck, Leary Murphy, Jerry Watts, Lynne Westfield, and Terry Todd, with special thanks to Steve Hilbun. We thank Nancy Noguera and Yong-sup Song for their assistance with translation.

Finally, we'd like to thank our editor at Pilgrim, Ulrike Guthrie, for her encouragement, advice, and patience, and her obvious commitment to the work of making the church a place where holy conversations can occur.

Introduction

The conversation about sexuality and the church is an opportunity extended to God's people. Often we are a church of strangers who have few authentic conversations about who we really are and our desires for our world. Yet, whether straight or lesbian, gay, bisexual, or transgender, we desire to be human together, to share our joys and our struggles.

Speaking out allows us not to feel alone. It allows us to connect with one another across differences and become the body of Christ. By choosing to be part of this study, you are taking action to enhance the body of Christ. To include yourself is an act of faith that God already includes you. We find God in one another and need one another to proceed down the journey of faith.

The Difficulty of the Discussion

This discussion may be a gift, but that doesn't make it any easier. One reason we have a difficult time talking about homosexuality is that we are uncomfortable with sexuality in general and sex in particular. We are saddled with traditions portraying sex and our sexuality as negative, dirty, and unspiritual. For some, sexuality is associated with a painful experience of rape or sexual abuse. Contemporary Western society exhibits an odd mix of attitudes about sexuality — it is both sex-obsessed and sex-denying. Sexuality is both something to be exploited and something about which we may not speak in polite company. For others, there is a transcendent aspect in sexuality. They believe that sexual activity has the potential for profound interpersonal and spiritual connection.

Homosexuality as an expression of our sexuality is even less understood. Only in the last thirty years have the American Psychiatric Association and the American Psychological Association removed homosexuality from their lists of mental and emotional disorders and begun to consider same-sex orientation as "normal" as being left-handed — a way of being human that once was also routinely demonized.

> When I started the church it was out of that need or desire to do something to help people know their place in creation, their right to a place of worship where they are free and comfortable and don't have to masquerade as someone else.
>
> — *Rev. Carl Bean, founder of Unity Fellowship Church, predominantly made up of African American LGBT Christians*[1]

According to the Web site of the American Psychological Association, "Most scientists today agree that sexual orientation is most likely the result of a complex interaction of environmental, cognitive, and biological factors. In most people sexual orientation is shaped at an early age. There is also considerable recent evidence to suggest that biology, including genetic or inborn hormonal factors," plays a significant role in a person's sexuality.[2] Ongoing studies of the animal kingdom have documented same-sex sexual behavior in animal species, confirming that homosexuality is "natural" in that it occurs in both human and nonhuman animal species. Research showing that the vast majority of child molesters are heterosexual men has helped alleviate some fears and prejudices, and "studies comparing groups of children raised by homosexual and heterosexual parents find no developmental differences between the two groups of children in four critical areas: their intelligence, psychological adjustment, social adjustment, and popularity with friends."[3] Still, misinformation and charges of perversion continue to elevate the debate to shrill levels.

The Church's Struggle

While some struggle with the scientific definition of homosexuality, churches struggle with how to treat the gay, lesbian, bisexual, and transgender people already in their pews and those in leadership as clergy or staff. Ongoing conversations about sexuality and Christian faith provide ample evidence that faithful Christians disagree on matters of homosexuality:

- In 1978, a Presbyterian Church of America resolution said homosexuality was "not God's wish for humanity."[4]
- In 1984, the United Methodist Church (UMC) added a clause to their rules stating that "no self-avowed practicing homosexual shall be ordained." In 2000, it commissioned a series of dialogues throughout the church on "homosexuality and the unity of the church."[5]
- At its 1988 annual meeting, the Southern Baptist Convention passed a resolution stating that it deplored "homosexuality as a perversion of nature and natural affections" and passed condemning resolutions at almost every annual meeting throughout the 1990s on topics like same-sex marriage or homosexuals in the military.[6]
- In 1991, the United Church of Christ agreed to affirm, celebrate, and embrace the ministry of lesbian, gay, and bisexual persons, encouraging local denominational leaders to welcome and support their candidacy for ministry.[7]
- The Metropolitan Community Churches invite all people — gay, lesbian, bisexual, transgender, and heterosexual — to new life through the liberating gospel of Jesus Christ, and its mission includes confronting the injustices of homophobia, sexism, and racism.[8]
- In 2000, the United Church of Canada affirmed that human sexual orientations, whether heterosexual or homosexual, are

a gift from God and part of the marvelous diversity of creation, and resolved to advocate for the civil recognition of same-sex partnerships.[9]

• In 2000, a gathering of over a thousand Christians from the United States and Canada launched a new ecumenical "Welcoming Church" network supporting the full inclusion and affirmation of lesbian, gay, bisexual, and transgender people in ministry and local congregations.

The Value of Dialogue

Amid the disagreements about ordination and same-sex unions, some churchgoers are uncertain where their leaders stand on having a dialogue about homosexuality. As a result, many of us haven't been able to openly discuss issues we see in the news. Family members of a gay or lesbian person may feel conflicted or ashamed when confronted by homophobic remarks by their fellow members at fellowship hours. The lack of structured spaces to sensitively discuss such opinions, and the silences in churches fearing conflict has led many to believe that the conversation itself is off-limits. The desire for unity (even the superficial variety) at any cost drives the conversation underground and leads to mistrust, secrecy, and risk avoidance.

A review of denominational policies reveals that many church leaders encourage their members to keep an open mind and to study. However, denominations remain uncertain how to best facilitate such discussions. Bringing together opposing sides in large-scale debates has often failed to produce a "Christian" result, leading only to hurt feelings, entrenched positions, and feelings of moral superiority. One-time discussions among small groups have produced more encouraging results; however, it is difficult to develop trust and to risk deep levels of sharing in a short-term arrangement. Groups who make a long-term covenant to share with each other stand the best chance for truly listening, learning, and finding God's truth in their exchanges with one another. Many denominational statements encourage such holy conversations. For example:

- Lutherans see their task as responding to today's voices, issues, and challenges of sexuality. They call for "discerning conversations within the church to understand the Spirit's leading in this situation."[10]

- The Episcopal Church urges each diocese to "find an effective way to foster a better understanding of homosexual persons, to dispel myths and prejudices about homosexuality."[11]

- American Baptists call on their members to "explore the biblical and theological issues of human sexuality."[12]

Resources of Faith

In this study's discussion we use the resources of faith — scripture, tradition, experience, and reason — to examine our theological understandings of homosexuality. Scripture, tradition, and experience are understood as sources for theology, and reason is the tool used to aid us in examining the other three. These are the principles of discernment used in testing truth.[13]

These four organizing principles are used to discuss sexuality, sexual orientation, and God's will for individuals and the church. Experience, as both the lens through which we receive information and as a source of information, is reviewed in session 3. Scripture is the primary source of our faith and is examined in session 4. Tradition is discussed in session 5. Reason, as the tool we use to interpret these three sources of theology, is integrated into all the sessions.

Reason refers to our ability to organize our understandings of scripture, to test our experience, or to judge the relevance of tradition to our current situation. Reason must be carefully used in any disciplined theological work. Although God's grace surpasses the scope of human language and comprehension, it is reason that allows us to see, however dimly, through the mirror and to talk about God. Reason enables people to research information and process facts. It can lead people to think in different ways. Reason can be an incredibly valuable resource for changing our minds to meet new situations; however, it can also be used to rationalize our prejudices and exclude any information that does not confirm our beliefs.

> I think that folks are reluctant to look at where they contribute to oppressions. White gay people go right to "I'm oppressed as a white gay man," but they're not going to look at how they contribute to racism. I have to tend to my identity of being middle class; I need to look at how I contribute to classism and to what's happening with poor people.... It doesn't take away from whatever experience and pain I have as a Black lesbian, but I have to own up to it as well.
>
> — *Renee L. Hill, Episcopal priest*[14]

Although each of the three sources are studied in separate sessions, they cannot properly be separated from each other, for each informs the other.

Theological Reflection

We hope this study will help you to:

- grow more comfortable with open, free, informing communication about human sexuality and homosexuality.
- discover some tools to discuss any controversial topic, in this case sexual orientation and sex/gender identity.
- explore connections between religion and sexuality.
- become more open to the life stories of others.
- articulate your theological understandings and to theologically engage homosexuality.

This last goal is critical to our task and has application beyond this study, for the task of doing theology is central to our lives as the body of Christ. Theology requires that we live with some inevitable tension and incompleteness. Being in conversation with our tradition and with others involves living in and through conflict. And because we can never fully comprehend God with our minds, our human language, or our personal experiences of God, the work of theology is always inadequate and incomplete.

Yet, as a church, we are uncomfortable with this tension and incompleteness and seek to remove it. Some Christians resist theological exploration by choosing doctrinal rigidity and dogmatic creeds in which beliefs are fixed. Any critical evaluation of or diversion from these standards is labeled heretical. In some denominations, even the conversation and questions about such doctrines are considered suspect and are legislated against.

> I don't think of myself as a woman, I don't think of myself as a man. I say I'm a transsexual. But labels are like stones in a stream. They're good to cross the stream, but if you stay on them, you don't really go anywhere. Maybe the one label that I do like is, if someone asked me who I really as, I would say, "I'm a child of God."
>
> — *The Reverend Erin Swenson, white, Presbyterian marriage therapist*[15]

Other Christians attempt to reduce the tension by suggesting that we simply live and let live. This "anything goes" tolerance of each other's position leads to a relativism that encourages apathy, indifference, and theological illiteracy.

In this study we are advocating neither the adoption of dogmatic positions nor the uncritical acceptance of diverse views. Instead, we want you to grapple seriously with the doctrine and theological formations that ground us as Christians. We seek the truth in Jesus Christ who said, "I am the way and the truth and the life." We seek God's word for our time. We recognize that the human search for divine understanding is fraught with sinfulness; it is a fragile task we undertake. It is in the honest struggle with our fellow Christians that the body of Christ is made real and known. It is in the vulnerable sharing of our truths that the divine is manifested and we glimpse the way, the truth, and the life to which we are called.

Underlying Assumptions

Our underlying assumptions in this study include:

- Mutually pleasuring sex by consenting adults is a good thing — very good!
- LGBT (lesbian, gay, bisexual, and transgender) persons, their families, and heterosexuals all share the same sacred worth and are to be equally valued and loved.
- Different opinions can coexist in the same church if people are willing to listen to one another.
- Laypeople and clergy can work together to study scripture and think theologically.
- Risk-taking conversations are worth it.
- Racism and homophobia are interrelated.

Hidden Issues of Power

In our ethnically diverse and race-conscious society there are power issues inherent in such a discussion. The session exercises that we suggest help us to think about issues of power. An antiracist approach is intentionally included and racism is named as a concern in the study. Language translations sprinkled throughout the book are reminders of the multiple cultures (racial/ethnic groups) in our communities. When we try to be "color blind" we are usually only assuming a white audience or trying to avoid conflict. This study calls us not to reproduce these same patterns, which thereby cause even more painful divisions. Conversations with these assumptions about sexuality erase the presence of people of color who are lesbian, gay, bisexual, or transgender. We realize that in the church and the larger society, many of us who are white don't have a lot of experience in talking about or understanding issues of racial oppression and white privilege. Those of us who are persons of color don't often have such discussions in racially mixed gatherings. However, it is important that we push past such discomfort and together find ways to discuss our different experiences with racial discrimination, prejudice, and privilege, and the damage they have caused.

Important work for racial equality has been done in the civil rights movement, and while there are points of similarity in the nature of the struggle for racial equality and LGBT rights, there are also ways that analogies between them are not helpful. Simple generalizations and comparisons about oppression should be avoided. Although there isn't space in this book to thoroughly explore the differences, it's important to note that the historical experiences of oppression for communities of color (a problematic, overgeneralizing term) are not the same as the experiences of oppression for those who are lesbian, gay, bisexual, or transgender (who are white and persons of color).

The Gift of This Study

Since we believe so strongly that undertaking such a risky and theologically challenging conversation can be a gift for those engaged in the conversation and for the church as a whole, the format for each session follows a GIFT format: *Gathering, Informing, Focusing, and Taking note.* GIFT is more than a structure for continuity: it is a statement about this opportunity for discussion as a gift. Sexual orientation is not the first controversial topic the church has encountered, and it will not be the last. We must find ways to conduct biblical study, to review our history and tradition, to listen to our individual as well as our collective experiences, and to use our reason to inform our discussion of our differences. In this way, our theological reflections around controversial issues can nurture our faith and our life together.

Each session has exercises to enable honest reflection and dialogue. In addition, there are "Going Deeper" experiences offered to allow for further study. In some cases, the Going Deeper exercises offer more cutting-edge opportunities. Tailor each session to your needs and to the particular interests of your group.

Through prayer, scripture readings, group exercises, and individual journaling, each session explores how our faith experiences impact our theological task. In all this you will bring your reason to interpret and imaginatively process what you are learning.

A facilitator's guide is located at the end of the book to assist you through each session. To avoid common pitfalls, facilitators should review this guide before making decisions about what to include and how to lead. A glossary is also included to help define acronyms and unfamiliar terms; it also reveals the fluid and developing nature of language regarding sexual orientation and gender identities.

Session One

Can We Talk?

¿Por qué la gente está haciendo de esto un problema tan grande? (Why are people making such a big deal about this?)

Yo no soporto escuchar esa manera inmoral y poco cristiana de pensar. (I can't stand to hear that immoral and un-Christian way of thinking.)

¿Por qué esas personas no leen la Biblia? (Why don't those people read their Bibles?)

¿Por qué tenemos que discutir esas prácticas perversas que están contra las leyes de Dios? (Why should we discuss these perverse practices that are against God's laws?)

Estoy cansada de que la iglesia se mantenga examinando continuamente mi orientación sexual, como si yo no fuera otra cosa que mi vida sexual con mi compañera lesbiana. (I'm so tired of having my orientation dissected by the church as if all I am is my sex life with my lesbian partner.)

¿Por qué tenemos que pasar tanto tiempo en este asunto? (Why do we have to spend so much time on this issue?)

We've all heard these voices in our churches: voices of dissent, voices of concern, and voices of frustration. So how do Christians talk to one another about controversial topics?

Sometimes we don't "talk" as much as we "debate," and what is lost in the process is the thoughtful reflection on the theology of our opinions. How are our beliefs formed? How does dialogue

23

with others influence those beliefs? How do our beliefs shape our own actions?

It is tempting to discuss homosexuality as if it were simply an issue that can be objectively debated. However, it is important to remember that we are not just talking about an issue — people's lives are at stake, fellow Christians' lives are at stake. No matter how we feel about the inclusion of LGBT persons, they are already in the church — in our pews and in our pulpits. While many denominations seek to limit or exclude the participation of LGBT persons in the ministry of the church, the truth is that LGBT persons are part of the foundation of faith that has brought us to where we are. They are Sunday school teachers, lay speakers, organists, daughters and sons, persons sitting in the pews, and clergypersons.

> It may not be too much to claim that the future
> of our world will depend on how we deal with
> identity and difference.
> — Miroslav Volf, white, Eastern European theologian[16]

In the last ten to thirty years, some denominations have stated that homosexuality is incompatible with Christian teaching. Other denominations have national policies welcoming LGBT people into the full life of the church, but the reality on the local level is often very different. And other groups preach forcefully that gays must transform themselves into heterosexuals, or at the very least pledge never to engage in same-sex behaviors, in order to be real Christians. Even within those denominations that condemn violence and speak of the human rights of all people, there are incidents of gays and lesbians being removed from their leadership positions or shunned from their churches altogether. There are parents of LGBT folks who are taught to condemn their child's homosexuality in order to save them from hell. And there are those LGBT children of God, like Matthew Shepard or Sakia

Gunn, who are killed, and their killers, who sometimes claim Christian inspiration for such deeds.

In some of our faith communities that are Korean, Native American, African American, or Latino, we pretend we don't have any LGBT persons in our midst. Or we pretend that we can't afford the energy to deal with sexual orientation issues and sex/gender identity issues in addition to being united in fighting white racism. In some of our predominately white congregations, there is a fear that acknowledging the presence of homosexuals might mar our image of being the "good, status quo group" in the community. There are multiracial congregations that feel over-burdened by diversity issues and are hesitant to add "one more difference" to their plate. And there are churches focusing on social justice issues such as poverty and homelessness, that con-sider sexual orientation discussions as an annoying divergence from the "real" ministry of the church. One of the struggles is to move beyond the us vs. them mentality (in whatever form it arises) that prevents us from finding the interconnections between homophobia and other forms of oppression. We must examine our model of scarce resources that abandons work on the bigger pic-ture to focus on only one issue. We need to recognize how our ministry and faithfulness are enriched by the conversation.

How can those with opposing viewpoints sit in the same room, much less converse on a topic that is, for many, about life or death? By coming together as part of the one body of Christ. Each person must bring a genuine openness to hear other people's stories. As a group you intentionally covenant to listen to one another and be open to God calling you to confess, to acknowledge your vulnera-bility, and to build trust with your fellow participants. Your whole group must be willing to agree to some basic guidelines that will govern your discussions. Exercise 2 offers a set of guidelines that can be a starting point for your group.

This first session offers you a chance to consider the power issues inherent in such a conversation. Who is included in the conversation? Who isn't able to join the discussion? Who gets to decide how people are included? These concerns will resurface in a later session when tradition is discussed and we examine whose ideas are written down, what is recorded as history, and what is included in our most common understandings of faith tradition.

GATHERING

Building trust, recognizing similarities amid differences, and opening ourselves to the lives of others forms the foundation for discussions about difficult topics. Conversation becomes holy when we invite God to be a part of it, when we recognize God's will for reconciliation with our neighbors and intentionally covenant with each other to bring our true selves to the discussion.

> The pastor of a church who had a large counseling service to help gays and lesbians change their sexual orientation believed homosexual behavior was an "abomination in the nostrils of God." He said: "It was done out of love and concern, but I have since concluded that those efforts were largely misdirected. If we have to err, isn't it better to err on the side of being too inclusive rather than being too exclusive?"
>
> — *The Reverend Alvin O. Jackson,*
> *African American pastor, Washington, D.C.*[17]

We invite you to create safe space where individuals can share the deepest parts of their life and faith. This is not always easy. In many parts of the country, LGBT people cannot fully share their lives due to the discrimination and danger they may face by sharing this information. For many persons, there are very real consequences to coming out, including losing jobs or ordination credentials. For men and women who have been abused, some discussions about sexuality may be painful or impossible. *Be aware of these dynamics in your group. Allow for silence and give permission for people to "pass" when sharing does not feel safe.* Assume that there are LGBT persons (or their parents or siblings) in your midst even if you are unaware of who they might be.

Opening Prayer, Scripture, and Song

Together read aloud the following scripture passage and prayer:

> I beg you to lead a life worthy of the calling to which
> you have been called, with all humility and gentleness,
> with patience, bearing with one another in love.
> — Ephesians 4:1–2

Holy God, who is known to us in the body of Jesus, help us to know

- our bodies,
- our sexuality,
- our sexual orientation, and
- our sexual identities as good gifts from you.

You have made us as deeply relational beings. Help us

- to listen attentively to our lives,
- to discern the leaning of our hearts,
- to hear the pain and joy of others, and
- to see the connections between others' experiences and our own.

Help us use the power of touch to heal and not harm,
the desire to connect to build up and not tear down,
the passion of bodies to love and not to hate. Amen.

Sing "Jesu Tawa Pano" (Jesus, We Are Here), or a Taizé tune such as "Veni Sancte Spiritus," or another meditative piece of music that can center your energies on Christ's presence within the conversation. Try to use a piece that is not in English, or one that is from a culture other than the majority culture of your group to remind participants that the Word is not the exclusive territory of any one culture.

Exercise 1: Introductions (Facilitator's Guide, page 131)

Let's get to know each other better.

Step One:

Introduce each other by dividing into pairs. Spend five minutes sharing briefly with one another about yourself, including two unusual tidbits of information that everyone else is unlikely to know.

Step Two:

After a few minutes, return to the larger group. Each person introduces their partner by sharing three pieces of information about that person (in addition to their name). Two pieces of information should be truthful and one should be concocted.

Step Three:

After each introduction, let the group guess which piece of information is false.

> To be honest, I'm tired of it. I'm tired of having my faith and my ministry questioned because I'm gay. I have learned that the support offered by the church is not trustworthy. I have learned to make sure I place my faith in God, not in the church.
>
> — Mark Johnston, pastor and psychiatric counselor,
> *Disciples of Christ clergy, racial/ethnic identity unknown*[18]

Exercise 2: A Covenant for Discussion

(Facilitator's Guide, page 132)

As a group of people about to embark on a very personal theological journey, a covenant is a helpful way to provide agreed-upon guidelines that can facilitate conversation and deepen trust.

Step One:

Reread the section in the Introduction entitled "The Value of Dialogue" (page 16).

Step Two:

Review the following ground rules and choose which of these your group will honor. Add any additional guidelines your group wants to follow.

1. Be as authentic as possible, but do not assume this is a safe place to share information that might jeopardize your job or mental health.

2. Make an agreement consistent with the group's concerns about confidentiality and how the information shared within the group will be communicated outside of the meetings. You may want to agree that no one can share someone else's comments outside the group.

3. Agree to listen respectfully and completely by not interrupting each other or speaking repeatedly without having heard all the participants.

4. Respect differences of opinion by using "I" statements ("I have experienced . . .") rather than characterizing someone else's experience or judging it. Speak from your own experience or understandings and do not project your own experience as normative.

5. Give each other permission to experience conflict with one another and remain a part of the group anyway. Don't try to smooth over differences or seek quick resolutions. Instead, affirm that we're all on the journey together and that part of

the value of the study is learning how to be in conflict with one another.

6. Do not attack, dismiss, or demean others, and guard against character assassinations or name-calling.

7. Do not assume that everyone in the room is heterosexual. Some gays and lesbians need to remain closeted, and some parents or siblings of gays or lesbians may be hesitant to share this information. Some may still be questioning their sexual orientation.

8. Include your heart in the conversation instead of focusing only on the head. Bring your whole self to the discussion — your emotions, imaginations, spiritual insight, and vision.

Are there other guidelines your group wants to affirm?

Step Three:

Consolidate the agreed-upon guidelines onto newsprint.

Step Four

Each person should sign the newsprint as a sign of commitment to the covenant. Post the covenant at each meeting.

Expect Discomfort (Facilitator's Guide, page 133)

As an introduction to the next activity, read the section in the introduction titled "The Difficulty of the Discussion" on page 13. Discussing sexual orientation, sexuality, and sex in general is difficult, uncomfortable, and most likely unusual in a church setting. Acknowledge your discomfort and commit yourself to hanging in there.

Exercise 3: Pictionary (Facilitator's Guide, page 133)

Step One:

Divide into two teams.

Step Two:

The facilitator will provide each team with a word for a volunteer from the team to "draw," allowing one minute for the rest of the team to guess the correct answer. You may not use letters or numbers in the "picture" drawn to represent your team's word. Each team takes turns drawing one of the words provided by the facilitator listed in the facilitator's guide. (Participants: don't peek!) Note: The words have been chosen to elicit fun and also increase your comfort level with discussing sexuality themes.

INFORMING

While each of the three resources of theology — scripture, tradition, and experience — will be examined separately in a future session, it is important to at least provide an introduction to the terminology at this point. As a tool for examining all of the other sources, reason will be woven into all the sessions.

Exercise 4: Resources of Faith (Facilitator's Guide, page 133)

It is important to acknowledge how our understandings of the four resources impact our ability to use them to discuss anything, especially a topic as fraught with potential fear and conflict as sexuality. When we recognize the roles that scripture, experience, tradition, and reason have played in our personal histories of Christian faith, we notice the negative or positive connotations attached to each. Then we can better understand their use in our own conclusions about what is true and what is not. For example, if tradition has always been used to oppress me as a transgender person, then I am less likely to value it as a source of discernment. Or if scripture has always been a source of comfort for me, then I may find healing there for the pain, trauma, and rejection that current policies inflict on me, as, for instance, the parent of a gay son.

Brief definitions of the four resources:

Experience: The lens through which we receive information

Scripture: The primary source for our faith

Tradition:	The way theological understandings are maintained
Reason:	The mental capacity used to interpret, organize, and test experience, scripture, and tradition

Step One:

Divide into four groups. Each group should briefly brainstorm words associated with one of four resources of faith (scripture, tradition, experience, and reason — assign one per group).

Step Two:

Review the brainstormed words. What do these words or images reveal about the task of creating Christian theology?

Step Three:

How do these words or images inform our theological understandings of sex, sexuality, and homosexuality?

I don't come to the scriptures with a "tabula rasa" (a blank slate). I come with some kind of experience either positive or negative, which colors my reading of scripture and is likely to predetermine the outcome. My experience causes me to look for an interpretation of the scriptures that satisfies and confirms how I feel as a result of my experience. And the same is true of tradition and reason. I can find traditional and rational grounds to back up whatever conclusion I have arrived at based on my experience.

— Jack M. Tuell, white, United Methodist bishop[19]

Exercise 5: How Do We Discuss Sexuality? What Is It?

(Facilitator's Guide, page 133)

The church has historically done a poor job of discussing sexuality in general, much less sex/gender identity or sexual orientation. As debate about the full inclusion of LGBT persons in church and society surfaces conflicting views, it is important to try to have a common understanding of sexuality — what it is and what it is not.

Can we contemplate a definition of sexuality that encompasses a broad understanding of our incarnate, sexual selves, including, but not limited to, sexual acts?

Since "sexuality" is a richly evocative term, subject to a wide variety of definitions and interpretations, the goal is not to reach one definition but to encourage you to consider your own definitions and ideas about sexuality. After sharing your ideas and hearing the views of others, you may adjust or enlarge your original concept.

Step One:

Read the following quotations and record the words or phrases that catch your attention.

- "Sexual references are pervasive in our society, but that doesn't mean sexuality is widely discussed and well understood."[20]

- "Human sexuality is what provides men and women with the capacity to enter into relationships with others. Sexuality is that dimension of humanity that urges relationships. Sexuality thus expresses God's intention that we find our authentic humanness in relationship."
  — Kelly Brown Douglas, African American theologian[21]

- "Our sexuality is intrinsic to the divine-human connection."
  — James B. Nelson, white ethicist[22]

- "Our sexuality — our way of being in the world as embodied selves, male and female — involves our whole being, and is intrinsic to our dignity as persons. Sexuality expresses the wonder of knowing that we are created by God with a need and desire for relationship. We are created for communion and communication. As sexual persons, we reach out for the physical and spiritual embrace of others. In our capacity to touch and be touched, we experience God's intention that we find our authentic humanness, not in isolation, but in relatedness." — Presbyterian study[23]

- "Human sexuality was created good for the purposes of expressing love and generating life, for mutual companionship and pleasure. Yet it has been marred by sin, which alienates us from God and others. This results in expressions of sexuality that harm persons and communities."

  — Evangelical Lutheran Church[24]

- "Sexuality is a central life force — it is related to our genitals, but is not limited to them — it also includes:

  - our emotions,

  - our presence and affect (what happens when we enter a room),

  - our physical bodies (how they are shaped, their texture — hairy or smooth)

  - our senses (how we taste, smell, hear, see and touch)

  - how our bodies are 'abled' (their stamina, flexibility, skill at pleasuring)"

    — Traci West, African American ethics professor

- "Sexuality is God's good gift."

    — United Methodist *Book of Discipline*[25]

Step Two:

Consider what one general conclusion you can draw about sexuality from these quotations and share your insights with three people sitting nearby.

Step Three:

In the large group, share the similarities and differences of one another's general ideas. How do these differences and similarities make conversation about sexuality easy or difficult?

> The church's fundamental issue in the field of human sexuality can be named in two words: It is power and it is fear. That fear must be expunged from our church once and for all, and that power must be shared.
>
> — *Bishop Steve Charleston, Native American Choctaw, dean of Episcopal Divinity School, Cambridge, Massachusetts*

FOCUSING

How do we discuss scripture passages that continue to raise conflict in churches, families, and the broader society? How do we acknowledge the power issues inherent in such a discussion? In other words:

- Who gets included in the discussion?
- Which voices are silenced, by whom, and why?
- Which voices are more highly valued? Why?

To address some of this complexity, it may be helpful to read a few scripture passages that have historically been debated in church and society and at least acknowledge some of the risks involved when we bring together different perspectives.

Exercise 6: Risky Scriptures (Facilitator's Guide, page 134)

Step One:

For each of the following four scripture passages, read the text aloud. Listen to the text without comment. It may be hard to do

this. Also, it may be painful to hear these scripture verses. Take a
moment of silence after each reading to write down your responses
to the questions listed below.

Read Ephesians 6:5–6

- What is risky about having a conversation about this text?

- What are the risks to the relationships with one another in
  the group if this text is discussed openly? (For example: Is
  there someone whose African American ancestors may have
  been enslaved that may be offended by certain comments? Are
  there whites in the group who may feel shame or be annoyed
  because the subject of slavery is raised?)

Read Mark 10:2–12

- What are the risks involved in having a conversation about
  this text?

- What are the risks to the relationships with one another in
  the group? (For example: Is there someone present who is
  divorced and may feel hurt or judged by the statements that
  someone else might make? Is there someone there who may
  feel shamed and judged because their parents were divorced?)

Read 1 Timothy 2:11–15

- What are the risks involved in having a conversation about
  this text?

- How might the relationships with one another in the group be
  affected? (For example: Is there a church leader present who
  may not want to be part of a church with such a tradition?
  Is there a woman who does not have children who may be
  disturbed by some of the comments relating to the text?)

Read Romans 1:24–32

- What are the risks in having a conversation about this text?

- What are the risks to the relationships with one another in the
  group? (For example: Is there someone who is lesbian, gay, bisexual, or transgender who may feel demeaned or disappointed

by statements that are made by members of your group? Is there a parent, sibling, or family member of someone who is LGBT who may feel their loved one is being degraded?)

Step Two:

Divide into groups of three or four and share your impressions from hearing these texts. What are the dangers for the larger church when having conversations about these texts?

Step Three:

Return to the larger group and briefly share responses and concerns.

Exercise 7: Our Hopes and Fears (Facilitator's Guide, page 134)

We've talked about the range of topics that will arise during this study. Now let's talk about our hopes and fears for continuing our conversation.

Following the facilitator's instructions, record your answers to the following questions stationed around the room on newsprint:

1. What fears do I have about participating in this discussion?
2. What is one hope that I have for this study?
3. How might this conversation nurture my faith?
4. If someone in my family "came out" to me as homosexual, my response would be....

TAKING NOTE

Take a few minutes to further consider the question, "How might this conversation and study nurture my faith?" Journal your response.

Assignments for Next Session

1. Read Jay's story (page 40).
2. Read the introduction to session 2 (page 45).

3. During the next week, see how many times you can use the
   words "theology" and "sexuality" in the same sentence.

Closing Song

If there is time, end by singing a song together from your community's hymnal or song book that talks about the role of the faith
community in our spirituality (for example, "We Are the Church,"
"Blest Be the Tie That Binds").

Closing Prayer

Holy God, who knit us together in our mother's womb, who
calls us by name, and who includes us as children, we pray
for those here today and those who are absent, for those who
can speak and for those who are silent. We pray for those gay
persons of every ethnicity who feel uniquely challenged by
religious and cultural forces; for parents who guard the secret of their child's orientation — fearful of disgrace, scared
of being ostracized, ashamed of their silence; for transgender
persons living with the dissonance of what they know themselves to be and the body that is visible to the world; for
bisexual persons who feel misunderstood and excluded by
both straight and gay worlds; for those questioning their sexual orientation or sexual identity, who live with unbearable
uncertainty and social pressure to conform. We name the
silence, in this room and in our broader culture, which sometimes keeps us from knowing each other fully, from trusting
each other completely, from sharing our whole selves. We
invite Jesus to be our companion in our journey together
and a partner in our holy conversations. Amen.

Going Deeper: Upness

For men, sexuality is often reduced to sexual acts, which most
often means genital experience, and neglects intimacy and sensu-
ousness. James B. Nelson, professor and theologian in the fields
of Christian ethics and embodiment theology, includes some

observations about male sexuality in his book *The Intimate Connection: Male Sexuality and Masculine Spirituality.* The following observations are based on that list.

1. Men tend to be goal-oriented in sex, focusing on the orgasm.

2. Men often bear numerous concerns about their technical performance: Did I do well? Did I satisfy my partner?

3. Men have an unusual concern for living up to their images of "normal'" male sexual functioning and are terrified by the thought of "not being a real man."

4. Men believe they must be in charge.

5. Men feel responsible for orchestrating the lovemaking and feel responsible for its "success."

These are, of course, generalizations, and some of them fit heterosexuals more than gays, but since many of them affect most men at least some of the time, Nelson examines three underlying issues: sexism, genitalization, and separation. His analysis suggests that male genitalization encourages externalization of mystery and seems to encourage men to prize the qualities of hardness, upness, and linearity. These things are not just part of the male sexual experience but a treasured and celebrated part of it. Erection is pleasure and potency, necessary for sexual "success," and the erection mentality is projected upon the world and what seems to be valuable in it. Consider hardness. In the male world of achievement, hard facts mean more than soft data. Men listen more readily to data from the hard sciences than to the soft, seemingly mushy information and theories of the behavioral sciences. Universities reward their physicians and physicists more amply than their humanities scholars. Consider upness. Computers are "up" when they are functioning, "down" when they are in trouble.[26]

- Would you agree or disagree with this generalized evaluation? Why?

Brainstorm ten items that are hard and ten that are soft. Are males or females associated with each of your items? Which items are more highly valued and why?

- Is it appropriate to pray to God about such things as orgasms, pleasing your partner, or about sexual function or dysfunction?

Going Deeper: The Folly and Fun of Getting to Know One Another

In groups of three or four, share with each other your responses to the following statements:

- The sexiest food in the world is probably...
- I think swimming on a nudist beach would be...
- When asked whether birds or fish are sexier, I always say...
- If somebody you just met at a party has a critical zipper open you should...
- The sexiest thing I know about geography is...

Going Deeper

Watch the movie *The Wedding Banquet,* a story of a clash of cultures when a gay man is visited by his Taiwanese parents who have a mistaken understanding of his sexuality.

ஃ JAY'S STORY

Jay is a white ordained minister in a mainline Protestant denomination. Born in 1958, Jay and his family moved to the San Francisco Bay area when he was a young child. His mother worked for a high-end department store's jewelry section. His father was an accountant. Jay is the youngest of three siblings, and the only son.

Jay notes that his family held to the traditions of the times: "Dad was a traditional dad — besides work, he was involved in

Masonic activities." There wasn't a lot of communication in the family. "Mom . . . had a black-and-white view of the world," which left little room for the give-and-take of ideas. Early on, Jay learned what was expected of him and what behaviors were acceptable. "It was all unspoken, but I knew what I could and couldn't share. I was a 'good boy' with a very dominant shadow side."

Jay wasn't the only one constricted by these unwritten rules of conduct. "My oldest sister had a lot of trouble with my parents and was banished from home at sixteen. She didn't play by the family rules, and that caused a lot of grief. That's how I learned not to be visible. I simply became what the family wanted to see."

This lack of honest communication led to a surprising discovery years later: "When my dad died, I discovered that he may have been gay. I was in seminary at the time, and I was coming back to California for my church's annual meeting. He died the night before I left seminary. He had parked in the Polo Fields in San Francisco at a time when it was very cruisy. He had a heart attack while on the trails. I found a gay novel in a brown paper sack underneath his car seat. It filled me with great sadness that I never knew who he really was. In reflection years later, I realized that I did not want to be anonymous like my dad. I yearned to be visible, authentic, and faithful to whom God created me to be."

Jay recalls that his family was quite active in a local church when he was a youngster. But after a falling out with the minister, his parents stopped attending. "I continued to go, even though I was very young — maybe seven or eight — at the time. Eventually, I made it over to another church. My sister had visited this church for a Job's Daughters event, and encouraged me to go. There was a desire, a need, and a connection for me there. Eventually, it became my home church."

Jay became more and more involved in the life of the church. Eventually, Jay realized he was being called into ordained ministry: "I was involved in Boy Scouts. I became an Eagle Scout and worked at a Boy Scout Summer Camp where I had my calling. My calling was something gradual that was always a part of me,

but it crystallized at the summer camp. I was fifteen or sixteen at
the time."

It was also during this time that Jay met his future wife, and they
began to date. This relationship continued all through college.
Following college, they were married. After returning from their
honeymoon, they packed up and moved to the Midwest, so that
Jay could attend seminary. The couple later adopted two children.
By all appearances, their lives seemed fine, except Jay was holding
a secret that was becoming increasingly difficult to hide:

> In hindsight, being honest with myself, I realize I was gay
> all my life, but I was so caught up in the traditional role
> of the minister. It wasn't safe to be fully who I was. Who
> I was called to be got really blurred as I tried to fulfill the
> expectations of the church and tried to be true to who I was.
> I couldn't be fully honest with myself, let alone anyone else.

For a long time, Jay tried to maintain a balance between his public
life and his personal self, "but I couldn't. I needed to be honest
with myself, my family, and come out as fully who God intended
me to be."

Eventually, Jay knew that he had to end his marriage. "Separating from my wife was like a death, and it was the crux of
owning my own sexuality. By not being honest, with my wife and
with myself, I realized I had been hurtful unknowingly. Through
therapy I was able to discover how split I was, leading the double
life of what others expected of me and who I really was, and then
began the merging of the two."

This integration of the personal and public has not been quick,
nor is it complete. Six years later, Jay recognizes that "there are
times when I continue to be split because the church continues to be not fully inclusive." Even as a youth, Jay realized that
the church was not inclusive. "I can remember a conversation
between the pastor and a layperson around the issue of homosexuality and youth groups. They would be welcomed here, but
they wouldn't be put in a leadership position (this was in the early

1970s). It was one of those experiences where I knew something wasn't right, but I couldn't respond; it was unsafe."

Even though scripture "was basic in the churches I grew up in," Jay reflects that there were some parts of scripture that were not included in public worship: "I never heard a sermon on the Song of Solomon; sexuality was not really preached about. It was omitted. Even youth group didn't talk about sexuality, even relating to scripture." The underlying message Jay received was "to be traditional. Women and men were to be married, that was what was appropriate and considered scriptural."

By coming out as a gay man and breaking out of the tradition that was imposed on him, Jay "began to see scripture in a new way. The scriptures became personal when I became real. They began to make sense as I grappled with tough issues." As a result of his own encounter with scripture, Jay tries to teach his congregation that "there is more than one way to interpret scripture. In my preaching, I look at more than one resource to understand what is being said in scripture. I don't preach only one viewpoint but offer to my congregation the fact that we are not of one mind, whatever the issue or text."

It is in honest struggle with the variety of faith experiences and biblical interpretations that essential truths emerge: "Discernment is necessary to see how tradition relates to us in this moment rather than holding tight to the tradition of an earlier era. When a community really engages text and tradition with honesty, openness, and vulnerability, we see God's spirit more clearly."

By integrating his public and personal selves, a healthier person has emerged, which has informed his pastoral vocation:

When congregational relationships are based on trust and openness, we can be more honest about who we are. When fear dominates, this is not possible. In scripture, we always hear the faith stories that start out in fear. When we overcome that fear, we come to the other side and step forward in faith. If Moses had allowed fear to prevent him from interacting with the burning bush, the Israelites might still be wandering in the wilderness. If Jesus hadn't touched the leper or interacted with the Samaritan or if he had allowed the fear of social norms to dictate his ministry, we would still be very stuck as a people of faith. We need to overcome our own fear in order to take a step of faith and allow each other to be who God created us to be.[27]

Session Two

Are We Theologians?

The task of every Christian is to engage in thoughtful reflection about his or her Christian faith utilizing the resources of scripture, tradition, and experience and engaging the tool of reason. When we do so, we are *doing* theology. Theology, simply put, is God-talk. It is what we believe to be true about God, God's relationship with and purpose for creation, and our relationship with God.

Everyone does it. Consider this childhood hymn:

Jesús me ama. Lo sé porque la Biblia asi me lo dice.
Los más pequeños le pertenecen, ellos son débiles, pero él
    es fuerte.

Jesus loves me this I know, for the Bible tells me so.
Little ones to him belong, they are weak but he is strong.

When children sing this hymn, they are stating a theology ("Jesus loves me") that stems from their own experience ("This I know"). It emerges from the Bible ("for the Bible tells me so"), and is upheld by church tradition which has passed along this song to many generations of preschool children. That is what theology is all about!

Many of us were raised to believe that there are other, wiser minds than ours to whom the work of theology should be entrusted. Any faith questions we had were to be answered by the experts: clergy, Sunday school teachers, and theologians. We believe that theology is best and most authentic not when it's handed down by those in authority and power but when it bubbles up through the lives, loves, and experiences of God's people.

Too often, the theology of a few becomes the doctrine for the many. Those in power (yes, even in power in the church) often try to universalize their theological understandings based on their own scholarly encounter with scripture, wrestling with tradition, and personal experience. Then the theologies of nonpowerful people are omitted at the expense of a fuller understanding of God and human community, which is why we believe that conversation is so central to the task of theology. Conversation allows for the give and take of thoughts, experiences, reflections, and ideas. As we engage in holy conversation with others, particularly those who differ in life experience and background, we are enriched by their wisdom and knowledge. Together, we formulate a theology of greater depth and breadth than we could ever realize separately.

> I was really interested in the Christian group on campus. I was intrigued by what they were saying about Jesus, that I could have a personal relationship with him. I wanted that! So I began attending their fellowship meetings, reading the Bible, and working on my relationship with Jesus. It was a very exciting time for me! But then they started telling me I was getting it all wrong, showing me what my personal relationship with Jesus was supposed to look like. I left that group and never looked back.
>
> — Carrie, twenty-four-year-old white lesbian graduate student

Theology is not only expressed in the religious sphere of our lives together. People use God's name in a variety of public settings. God's name is invoked before many high school sporting events, at national remembrance rituals (like Memorial Day ceremonies), and the "christening" of new ships. Consider these common familiar U.S. patriotic sayings:

God bless America

In God we trust

One nation under God

What is the theology behind "God bless America"? Are we asking God to bless America and withhold blessings from other countries? What kind of blessing is being requested? What's the theological message when God's name is invoked in a country whose diversity includes people of many faith traditions as well as people who have no belief in God? Whose God is being invoked? It is important that we are mindful of the individual and collective ways we do theology.

As the global village shrinks and we recognize our connectedness beyond national boundaries, we must be critical of the ways individual countries use theology to promote nationalism. As we place our faith in God, in whom there is no east or west, how can we ensure that the theology articulated in the public square helps us to recognize our interrelatedness?

Remember that our culture is like an eyeglass lens through which we develop our theology. How we understand God and a faithful lifestyle is always rooted in our cultural DNA. Consider these two different interpretations of the opening verses of Psalm 23, both rooted in a specific cultural context:

The Lord is my programmer,
I shall not crash
He installed his software
in the hard disk of my heart;
all of his commands are user-friendly.
His directory guides me to the right choices
for his name's sake. — Author unknown[28]

The Great Father above a Shepherd Chief is
I am His and with Him I want not.
He throws out to me a rope

and the name of the rope is love
and He draws me to where the grass is green
and the water is not dangerous,
and I eat and lie down and am satisfied.
Sometimes my heart is very weak and falls down
but He lifts me up again and draws me into a good road.
His name is Wonderful. — George Hunt (Kiowa)[29]

These versions of Psalm 23 show vividly how culture, language, and experience impact one's theology. For all our attempts otherwise, theology is rooted in the culture that articulates it. Theology seeks to shape culture at the same time it is being shaped by culture. A part of our theological task is to provide meaning within our own cultural context while at the same time acknowledging the cultural context from which our theology is shaped.

Being in conversation with people who are unlike us can help, whether we have differences of race/ethnicity, class, sexual orientation, or sex/gender identity. It can help us broaden not only our worldview, but also our experience of God!

그녀는 마치, "너 한국사람이야???!!" 라고 하는 듯 했다. 그녀는 코리안 아메리칸이었고 동성애자가 아니었다. 내가 그녀에게 동성애자임을 밝혔을 때, 그녀는 계속해서, "너는 어떻게 한국인이면서 레즈비언일 수가 있어??! 네가 어떻게 한국인이라고 할 수 있어??"라고 물었다.

She was like, "You're Korean???!!" She was Korean American and straight. When I came out to her, she kept asking, "How can you be Korean and lesbian??! What do you mean you're Korean??"[30]

— *Patti, biracial, Korean American lesbian, Atlanta*

GATHERING

Let's prepare ourselves for this session through prayer, scripture, and song. You may choose to review last session's assignments before moving forward.

Opening Prayer, Scripture, and Song

(Facilitator's Guide, page 136)

In the last session, group members answered the following questions: "What fears do you have about participating in this discussion?" and "What is one hope that you have for this study?"

The facilitator has posted them on the walls. Use your responses to create an opening prayer.

Read 1 John 1:1.

The author uses the authority of his own faith community's experience as the starting point for this epistle. As you move through this session on theology, be aware of how you rely on scripture, experience, tradition, and reason to build your theology.

Sing a song from your community's hymnal or song book that talks about one's personal relationship with God (for example, "In My Life [Be Glorified]," "Spirit Song," "Every Time I Feel the Spirit").

In the last session the group covenanted to follow a collection of guidelines for the study. Review these guidelines. If there are any new members to the group, are they willing to enter into the group's covenant? Invite them to sign their name(s) to the list.

Today's Theme — Popcorn Style (Facilitator's Guide, page 136)

When you read the introduction to this session, what phrase or idea caught your attention? Share the phrase with the rest of the group. No explanations are needed. Just let the ideas jump out . . . like popcorn!

As you find ways to express your beliefs during this study, our hope is that you will, in the words of feminist theologian Nelle Morton, "hear each other into speech" and create safe space for one another to speak, wonder aloud, question, and disagree. In this way, we are led to a deeper understanding of ourselves, sex, sexuality, and God.

Exercise 1: I Have Permission! (Facilitator's Guide, page 136)

Give yourself permission to speak your theology, today and throughout this study, knowing that your thoughts, like you, are a work in progress. Fill in the blank, and give yourself permission!

I, _____, hereby have permission to be imperfect with regard to human sexuality. It is okay if I don't have all the answers or if, at times, my ignorance and misunderstandings become obvious.

I have permission to be embarrassed as we talk about things I was brought up to believe are private. I have permission to ask questions that appear stupid. I have permission to struggle with these issues and be honest about my feelings.

I am a product of a homophobic culture that is both sex obsessed and sex denying, and I am who I am. I don't have to feel guilty about what I know or believe, but I do need to take responsibility for what I can do now:

- Try to learn as much as I can.

- Struggle to change inaccurate beliefs and oppressive attitudes.

- Respect others as they learn and grow.

  Signed,

_____

Exercise 2: Ages and Stages of Faith Development
(Facilitator's Guide, page 137)

Does our understanding of God and faith change over time? Take a few moments to fill in the boxes on the following page.

Step One:

Choose two distinct periods from your life and write down the ages in the space provided. Then think back to what you believed during that time and answer the questions for each age period.

Age: _____

My fundamental belief about God:

_____

Primary role of the believer:

_____

Where the faithful community was found:

_____

Age: _____

My fundamental belief about God:

_____

Primary role of the believer:

_____

Where the faithful community was found:

_____

Here's an example:

- Age: 10

  - My fundamental belief about God: God is love
  - Primary role of the believer: To be a "good girl"
  - Where the faithful community was found: Sunday school

- Age: 24

  - My fundamental belief about God: God is a God of mercy and justice
  - Primary role of the believer: To work for justice
  - Where the faithful community was found: Progressive churches and peace marches

Step Two:

After you have finished filling in all the blanks, move into small groups and share your responses.

Step Three:

Move back into the large group and discuss the following points:

1. Did your faith understandings remain the same or change throughout your lifetime?
2. Looking at your understanding of God and faith, would you call yourself a theologian? Why or why not?
3. As Christians, we are called to reflect prayerfully on what we believe and what we know about God. Each of us, then, is a theologian!

Going Deeper: What Do We Know about God?

We worship a God of Many Names. Each name is a theological statement about the nature of God. For instance, when we invoke God's name as "Healer," we are making a statement about God as the source of human wholeness. "Bread of Life" communicates a theology of the sustenance God provides. Below are examples of names of God. What kind of theological statement does each name imply?

Breath of Life: _____

Creator: _____

Rock of Ages: _____

Lover of My Soul: _____

Divine Ecstasy: _____

Holy Laughter: _____

- What names do you use for God?
- Which names can you recall being used in worship at your church?
- Should unfamiliar names for God be used in worship? Why or why not?
- How does our own understanding about God change as we encounter another's understanding about God?

INFORMING

The above exercise revealed how our theology changes over time. Not only do our individual theologies change, but the theology of communities (small groups, local congregations, denominations) changes over time as well. New understandings place a demand on every Christian to enter into theological reflection. What is God's Word for us in this time and place? How do we believe God is speaking to us? What new truth is God revealing to us?

In 2003, the Canadian government declared that it is illegal to withhold marriage from same-sex couples and began moving toward the federal legalization of same-sex relationships. In a press release following this declaration, the United Church of Canada's spokesperson, the Reverend Jackie Harper, described the church's changing understanding of sexuality:

God's intention for all human relationships is that they be faithful, responsible, just, loving, health giving, healing, and sustaining of community and self. . . . The implication is that these standards apply to both heterosexual and homosexual couples. The United Church seeks to support the diversity of families who uphold a secure environment for nurture, growth, and development and that will contribute to the spiritual, social, psychological, sexual, physical, and economic wholeness of the members. It is the experience of the United Church that non-traditional family forms equally advance these family values.[31]

In the United States, the issue of marriage equality has created a political tug-of-war in state legislative debates and ballot referendums, as well as in national election campaigns.

Meanwhile, many U.S. Protestant denominations are still debating holy union ceremonies for same-sex partners. They struggle to understand God's Word for our time as we learn more about the nature of homosexuality and the desire all persons have for loving and lasting relationships.

This debate is not the first time the church has rethought its stance about marriage. The many changes created by the Reformation included a new understanding of clergy and marriage. Prior to the Reformation, Protestant clergy were to be unmarried and celibate, but following the Reformation, they were allowed to be married. In the 1800s, most white U.S. churches forbade pastors from performing marriage rites for African slaves. When slavery was abolished, clergy were not permitted by the state to perform marriage rites for interracial couples because they were seen as unnatural unions.

In each of these situations, the relationship between the church and the broader culture is central to the emergence of new theological understandings.

Exercise 3: I Believe ... (Facilitator's Guide, page 137)

Each of us already has a theology of sexuality, an understanding of how God intends us to embody sexuality in a way that is biblically rooted and faithfully expressed. Our theology of sexuality today has probably undergone revisions over the years, even if we have not been conscious of the changes.

Step One:

Take a few moments to write a one-sentence statement of faith about sexuality.

For example, you could start your statement with:

I believe that sexuality is a good gift from God that is for ...

Or

I am not sure if sexuality is a good gift from God, but I do believe ...

Or

I believe God creates us to be in relationship and ...

Or

I believe God created my body for ...

Step Two:

If you are comfortable doing so, share your statement of faith in small groups. Then answer the following questions:

- What did you learn from hearing others' statements?
- Was there anything you heard that challenged you?

Step Three:

Is it possible to write a joint statement of faith about God's good gift of sexuality? Why or why not?

FOCUSING

Each of us brings our theology into the larger faith community to which we belong. When our differing theologies encounter one another, a new insight can emerge, new questions may arise, or conflicts can develop. What spiritual resources help us remain in relationships with those whose theologies differ from our own?

Exercise 4: Playing at a Church Council Near You
(Facilitator's Guide, page 137)

For this exercise, let's focus on issues of sexuality and theology that can arise in a local church meeting.

Role-play situation: The youth group director is aware that some of the youth are sexually active. Some are heterosexual, and some are gay and lesbian. Since the denomination believes that sexuality is a good gift, the youth director would like to teach several sessions on sexuality, including a session on safer-sex that includes information for same-sex partners. The council has received some complaints about the upcoming sessions, particularly about the safer-sex session. They are deciding whether or not the youth director should be allowed to teach that session.

Step One:

Divide the group into two: council participants and observers. Read the instructions for your group only. Then role-play the church meeting for about ten minutes.

Council participants: Think about what opinions your character might have on the safer sex session, as well as sex in general.

Youth director: You agree that sexuality is a good gift from God. You are concerned about the number of church youth — straight, gay, and lesbian — who are sexually active.

Pat: You believe the body is a temple and that sex is a gift meant to be shared within the marriage relationship.

Juan: You believe the church ought to be concerned with spiritual matters, not about sex or sexuality.

Kyung-Lee: You are the parent of a teenage daughter who uses birth control pills.

Terry: You are a parent struggling to understand a teenage son who has just revealed that he is gay.

Lou: You are the church council chair.

Council observers: As the role-play is occurring, consider these questions:

- Where did you see God present in this discussion?
- In what nonverbal ways did you see God at work?
- In what theological ideas did you hear God's voice?
- What voices of culture were present (for example: pop culture, ethnic, regional)?

Step Two:

When the role-play is over, observers should discuss their responses to the questions above.

Step Three:

For the entire group: Discuss the following questions.

1. Were there times when what was being discussed embarrassed you?
2. Were there cultural or theological assumptions that prompted the embarrassment?
3. Did one position prevail in the meeting? Why or why not?
4. Which voice was valued more highly (for example: popular, moralistic, ethnic, regional, church, God's)?
5. Whose voice was missing from the discussion? How might the conversation have been different if teenagers had been participating in the meeting?
6. How did the participants draw on spiritual resources for the meeting? Did they sit in prayer together? Did they refer to scripture at any time?

Theology should inform culture — not just through what we think but also through what we *do*.

TAKING NOTE

Offer each other a few moments of silence to answer the following questions in your journal:

1. How has your faith informed your understanding of sexuality?
2. What were instances in your life when you had wished the church had given you better guidance about sex and sexuality?

Sing a song from your community's hymn or song book about the varying gifts in the Christian community (for example: "Many Gifts, One Spirit," "Help Us Accept Each Other").

Assignments for Next Session

1. Research another tradition: Do a Web site search on what other denominations have to say about sexuality and homosexuality and compare with your own denomination. A good starting point is www.religioustolerance.com. Or, if you do not have access to a computer, find a few friends or neighbors who are laypersons in two church traditions other than your own and ask them what the official teachings of their church are, if any, on issues of sexuality and homosexuality. Do they agree with their denominational stance or not? If no teachings exist, what do they think their church's view should be?
2. Read the introduction to the next session (page 59).
3. Video: Check to see if your video store has the movie *Ma vie en rose* (*My Life in Pink*), a French film about a young boy who believes God made a mistake and he was really meant to be a girl. Rent it if you can (a great place to locate hard-to-find videos is www.netflix.com, which mails DVDs directly to your home).

Closing Prayer

Offer one-sentence prayers of thanksgiving for the ways God has made Godself known to you. Thank you, God, for the way you have enabled me to know you through _____ .

Session Three

Experience

The church was packed to overflowing. Flowers adorned the altar. The handbell choir was set up in the choir loft, ready to play. The women's guild had just put the finishing touches on the reception hall, and antsy children ran between the legs of adults. Finally, the music changed tone, and everyone turned expectantly to the back of the church. Down one aisle of the church came Michael; down the other, Sean. The two men stood before the minister, and the holy union officially began.

Such scenes were not unusual at Bethany United Methodist Church in San Francisco. The congregation is half LGBT, half straight. Here, young and old, LGBT and straight, rich and poor, African American, Chinese, Filipino, white, and Hispanic find a place of prayer and support, and the lives and loves of all members are celebrated and held up for blessing.

Children in this church have been surrounded by the care of adult members of the community — gay and straight — who have acted as Sunday school teachers, babysitters, mentors, godparents, chaperones, and friends. Older adults and younger parishioners, often separated from their families of origin by distance or family rejection, create strong bonds of friendship. Worship, in this community, becomes a weekly reunion of one's family of faith.

Imagine growing up in a church like this one. What does a child learn about love, about the role of community in one's life, about the significance of diversity, and about God in such a community? What are the explicit and implicit messages about faith that a child learns? How does children's experience of an intentionally inclusive community shape their theology and help them define themselves?

An important faith resource is experience. Experience emerges at the moment when our physical, intellectual, emotional, and spiritual selves intersect with the world. Look at a few examples of what we gain through experience:

- A musician who practices regularly gains skill through her experience.
- The experience of studying hard offers knowledge to the student.
- Watching a program about fire safety in the home gives homeowners new awareness about fire hazards in their home.
- Coming to terms with an HIV diagnosis, a patient discovers new truths about how to live purposefully.

"La experiencia nos va moldeando y transformando" (Experience shapes and molds us).

Factors that affect how we use reason to process experience include our cultural and ethnic backgrounds. These factors become a filter for our experience.

Several years ago, a junior-high church camp was held in the Sierra Mountains. As Bible study was being held underneath the trees, a large *boom* was heard. The adult counselors, mainly baby boomers, recognized the sound from their youth — a sonic boom from a military jet flying overhead. Today, the military is not permitted to break the sound barrier over populated areas. The youth, upon hearing the sound, dove to the ground. They associated the sound with a drive-by shooting, a not-altogether-infrequent occurrence in their communities. For both groups, the experience of the sonic boom was mediated by what was most familiar to them. The result was two very different responses.

Experience is an important resource for faith. God continues to make Godself known to the world. As we not only observe but live out our lives in the world, we have "God-moments," those experiences in which God's revelatory and salvific advances are made known to us. Experience helps clarify the intended meaning of scripture and tradition by testing possible interpretations.

But since each of us has our own unique experiences that inform scripture and tradition, how can we be sure we are faithful in our faith understandings? Using reason, how do we sort out experience, tradition, or scripture that at times seem contradictory?

Holy conversations are the key.

> We were getting ready to close our church. The congregation had dwindled to just a few old folks. The day of the vote, a group of young men came to church. They had so much energy and life! When they heard we were having a meeting after church, they went to the store and brought back food for a luncheon. There was so much life in church that day that we decided to postpone the vote. It turns out the men were homosexuals. We were surprised. Most of us had never met any homosexuals before. We certainly didn't expect to find them in our church. But as we got to know them, we really liked them! They weren't so different from us. Not only did we not close our church, the congregation grew as the homosexual men brought their friends to church. What a surprise!
> — *Mildred, an eighty-something white woman from Indiana*[32]

Gathering with others, particularly with those whose life experiences, ethnic and cultural backgrounds, class, educational level, and sexual orientations differ from our own, enables us to test our faith understandings through reason as our experience of God is enlarged by another's experience of God.

Too often, we discount the experience of certain people. This is particularly true of gay men, lesbians, bisexuals, and transgender persons in the church. While a lesbian may have had a profound experience of God's grace and saving power affirming of her life, her experience is considered invalid by those who feel that homosexuality is not compatible with Christian teaching. As long as she continues to embrace her lesbianism, her experience of God is seen as inauthentic. How would the debate regarding homosexuality change in our churches if the experiences of gay men, lesbians, bisexuals, and transgender persons were central to the conversation?

> My family and I faced so much prejudice during World War II. Even though we were born in the U.S., because we were of Japanese descent, we faced horrible treatment by people who had once been our neighbors. We were forced from our homes, we lost all our possessions, when we were sent to the camps. Seeing so many gay people rejected by their families reminds me of the pain of my own experience. I want my church to be a place where a gay person can be themselves and not be afraid of being turned away.
>
> — *Anna, seventy-six-year-old Japanese woman*
> *from San Francisco*

Sometimes, we affirm one part of people's experiences but then discount another part. In an all-black congregation, for instance, we may affirm the common history and cultural heritage of African American people that is so often ignored or devalued in the dominant society, but the struggle and cultural contributions of African American gays and lesbians are never named. In a church that is both predominantly (but not exclusively) white and LGBT, ignorance and devaluation of the history and cultural heritage of African Americans may prevail, but the church nonetheless offers spiritual nurturing by affirming the identity of church members as valued gay and lesbian children of God. How do we use reason to sort out what God calls us to be and do as God's people? How is this "sorting out" affected if the experiences of persons of color who are gay men, lesbians, bisexuals, and transgender are central in our discernment process?

GATHERING

Welcome one another to the meeting, and help each other prepare for the beginning of the session.

Opening Prayer, Scripture, and Song

In the book of Acts, Saul, a persecutor of Christians, has a religious experience that changes his life and outlook. Read in Acts 9:19b– 26 about how others felt about him and his experience.

For the opening prayer, pass around a lit candle. As you receive the candle, offer a one-sentence prayer of thanks for where and how you encountered God today.

Sing a familiar song or hymn about Christian experience (for example: "In the Secret," "I Come to the Garden," "Open My Eyes," "Spirit Song").

If you have time, you may choose to review the assignments from last time. What did you learn from your Web search or from talking to your friends and neighbors? What do other denominations have to say about sexuality and homosexuality? How does that compare with your own faith tradition? What surprised you? What angered you? What gave you hope? In the movie *Ma vie en rose* (*My Life in Pink*), what would you say was the theology of the child? How did the child know what he knew about God and gender?

Exercise 1: Do You See What I See? (Facilitator's Guide, page 138)

Step One:

Hold up the photo on the following page. Silently, take two minutes to reflect on the picture and answer the following questions:

1. What do you see?
2. What is happening in the picture? What is their relationship to each other?
3. How does it make you feel?

Step Two:

With the entire group or in small groups, share your answers. Then discuss:

- Are any of your experiences of the photo the same? Is there any wrong answer?

- Why do we often mistrust another's experience? To ponder further: What in your experience caused you to see what you did in the picture?

INFORMING

As the previous exercise demonstrated, events and experiences can carry multiple meanings as we filter them through our reason. How do we understand another's experience? What criteria do we use to determine the validity of another's experience?

Accepting another's experience as true is risky. We want to honor another's experience but also maintain some criteria for distinguishing what is real versus fictional. For instance, a child may think there are monsters in his closet. We listen to the child's fears while knowing that the monsters are the creation of the child's imagination.

For some of us who are LGBT Christians, our experiences are often similarly discounted or left out of church discussions

because others do not consider them to be authentic Christian experiences. What criteria are used to make this judgment? How can we ensure that we are not using reason to uphold biases and prejudices?

What makes for an authentic religious experience? These questions can provide some assistance:

1. Is the experience consistent with the gospel message of Jesus Christ, which seeks to increase our love of God and neighbor?

2. Does it result in behavior that is harmful to the dignity of self and others?

3. Does it result in behavior that enhances the well-being of self and others?

Judgments about another's experience are always subjective. God alone is the final arbiter. For this reason, we encourage holy conversations to help us learn from each other's experience.

Exercise 2: Authentic Experience (Facilitator's Guide, page 138)

Step One:

Consider these two religious experiences:

In 1738, John Wesley, the founder of Methodism, had a profound experience of the Holy Spirit which radically changed his life:

> In the evening, I went very unwillingly to a society in Aldersgate Street, where one was reading Luther's Preface to the Epistle to the Romans. About a quarter before nine, while he was describing the change which God works in the heart through faith in Christ, I felt my heart strangely warmed. I felt I did trust in Christ, Christ alone for salvation; and an assurance was given me that he had taken away my sins, even mine, and saved me from the laws of sin and death.

Clair realized she was a lesbian, but felt it conflict with her faith:

"I felt I had to choose: be gay or be with God. I didn't want to choose." Clair took a trip to Europe. Prior to her departure, she prayed, "I would like this question answered: 'Can I reconcile being gay with being a Christian? Can I be both at the same time?'" Clair arrived in London and checked into a youth hostel. One of the first people she met was a woman named Virginia from Massachusetts. "I saw that she had rainbow earrings. I wondered if she was gay. We went out to breakfast and talked about our travel plans. I asked her why she decided to travel by herself. She said, 'It wasn't by choice. My girlfriend couldn't make it because she was pastoring a church and couldn't take the time off.' I jumped up and cried and cried and cried. I was so elated. I told her, 'This was my quest: to reconcile being gay and Christian. And the first person I meet on my trip is a lesbian Christian applying for seminary, with a pastor as a girlfriend!'" That night, Clair prayed, "Okay God, I hear it. I guess there is a place for me."

Step Two:

Create two columns on newsprint. At the top of one column, write "Authentic" and on the other "Inauthentic." As a group, list why these experiences could be considered authentic or inauthentic religious experiences. Are there similarities between the two?

Step Three:

Were the criteria given at the start of this exercise helpful? Why or why not? What other criteria did you use? What role did reason have in your decisions?

Exercise 3: My Authentic Experience
(Facilitator's Guide, page 138)

Step One:

Think of a time when you had a profound experience of God. What led you to that experience? What did it feel like? How would you describe it to others? What are the distinguishing marks that make this an authentic religious experience for you?

Step Two:

Individually, create a poem that describes your experience of God.

> God
> [Three nouns describing God]
> [Four adjectives describing characteristics of God]
> [Two verbs describing actions of God]
> Me

For example:

> God
> Lover, Challenger, Liberator
> Compassionate, Fierce, Tender, Passionate
> Challenging, Holding
> Me

Step Three:

If you wish, share your poem with the group.

FOCUSING

Stepping out of our own experience and into the experience of another is a way to broaden our worldview and expand our knowledge about other people and the world in which we live. Can we gain a better understanding of how the dominant culture filters out the experiences of some people, while "normalizing" the experiences of others?

Exercise 4: Inside Out! (Facilitator's Guide, page 138)

Most of us grew up in a heterosexually dominated world. The customs and norms of the culture have influenced how we think and act. The gay or lesbian experience in this world is difficult for many of us to understand. The guided meditation on page 139 in the facilitator's guide is an opportunity for you to gain insight into the experience of gay men and lesbians in a heterosexually dominated culture.

At the conclusion of the exercise, we will take a few moments to discuss these questions:

1. What surprised you in this new world?

2. How did it feel to have heterosexuality seen as unnatural?

3. Was the world a fair place? For the disabled person of color? For the white gay person? For the gay parent of a straight child? Why or why not?

4. What did you learn from this meditation about the experiences of gay men and lesbians in our society?

TAKING NOTE

Journal your responses to the following questions:

1. How did you discover your sexual orientation?

2. Did you choose your sexual orientation or claim it?

3. How does your experience of your racial/ethnic background differ from your experience of your sexual orientation?

4. How does your experience inform the way you read scripture?

Assignments for Next Session

1. Read the introduction to the next session (page 74).

2. Read Clair's story (see below).

3. Experience Project: Do one of the following:

   • Find a gay newspaper and read it at your local coffee shop.

   • Go to your public library or bookstore and ask where you can find the gay/lesbian fiction center.

- Read the paper with new eyes: between now and your next session, count how many news stories, editorials, letters to the editor, or cartoons mention homosexuality.

Closing Prayer

Offer prayers of gratitude for the diversity of faith experiences represented in your group. Speak to God of the challenges and joys of living with so many different faith experiences.

❧ CLAIR'S STORY

Clair Chi is the daughter of immigrants: her father is from Cuba and her mother is from China. The two met through mutual friends after they both had moved to the United States. While Clair only has one sibling, a younger brother, she is surrounded by an extended family of grandmothers and aunts: "That was family to me."

In an era where latchkey children were the norm, Clair's parents made sure that there was always someone at home to care for them. "My mother worked at a bank, the graveyard shift. My dad was the manager of a shipping company and worked the day shift." Clair notes that there was a significant class difference between her parents. Money was a big issue. "Growing up, my mother was of working class, my dad was the owning class. My mother, in China, was always frantic making sure there was enough money for food on the table. You did what you needed to do to stay alive." Marriage, for Clair's mother, was a way to make sure the family would be economically stable. "My mother believed that a man was marriage material if he could make money and provide for the family. This was a major message I received growing up. I needed to marry someone who was well off. Love has very little to do with it."

The strain of these economic differences resulted in her parents seeking a divorce when Clair was in college. Besides class difference, Clair's parents also had different religious upbringings.

Clair's mother was a Buddhist, while her father was a Roman Catholic. Both parents believed that it was "important to give children a spiritual teaching, since it's the source of values and morality, of right and wrong." Clair recalls that "spirituality was a 'Dad and kids' thing, not Mom's." Clair and her brother were raised Roman Catholic. Her mother told her, "Since you're in America, you will go with the American gods. If we were in China, you would go with the Chinese gods." Clair soon became the spiritual advocate in the family. Each week, Clair would rouse her brother and father with "'It's Sunday, it's time to go to church.' I always took the initiative in getting my family to church."

Clair attended Catholic school through the eighth grade. Early in her education, Clair and her brother "were told we were speaking with an accent, so my parents were told not to speak Chinese to us at home." This message about assimilating to the dominant culture would be central to Clair's experience growing up.

Clair has many memories of trying unsuccessfully to fit in with her peers. "When I was young, clothes really defined the person. If you wore certain clothes, it implied that you had money and were in the 'in' crowd. I hated 'free dress days,' when we were allowed to wear whatever we wanted instead of the school uniform. I liked the fashions that the guys were wearing. They seemed so much cooler to me. But if you wore button-down Levi's, you were called a lesbian.

"I remember that in our seventh- or eighth-grade school picture, I was the only girl in pants. The cameraman said to me, 'Now smile, sonny.' He thought I was a boy, and I thought that was a great thing! But everyone else couldn't believe he had called me a guy, and they started shouting to him, 'She's a girl!'

"Being seen as a boy was exciting for me. It was really great, soothing. Girls were weak, bad at sports, petty, dependent. Boys were more adventuresome, a little on the rebellious side. They got to play with whatever they wanted. They had all the fun. The girls just sat on the bench not doing anything. When I was identified as a guy, I had a sense of place. I got to do the things that interested me.

"I went to public high school and thought that I could change the stigma of being a boy/girl. I went ultra fem, to prove to myself and others that I could be a woman."

Clair began to wear skirts and makeup, and had boyfriends. While she went through all the motions, she didn't understand the concept of "having feelings for someone, of falling in love. I had no emotional or romantic connections to boys. I felt I needed to wear certain clothes and do things with boys in order to be seen as a woman."

Even as she dated boys, she still had crushes on girls, and couldn't understand why. "I'd have these crushes and I would tell myself, 'Stop it! You aren't supposed to feel that. Get these feelings out of your head. Ignore them.'"

Clair found herself emotionally conflicted. She felt naturally attracted to women, but had to force herself to feel anything toward men. "I would keep pushing myself, 'Feel good. Be attracted [to him]. Try to kiss him. Make yourself do it.' But when I felt attracted to a woman, I would turn it off. . . . I wound up feeling very, very numb."

Clair could not name her feelings for women. As a young adult, she worked in an office and saw a picture of a woman on a coworker's desk. "When I asked her about it, she said it was her girlfriend! She was a lesbian! The first lesbian I knew, even though I lived in a gay-friendly city. I wound up having a huge crush on her."

Clair watched a movie on HBO that was pivotal to her self-acceptance. "I watched the movie *Bound*. I couldn't believe it when I saw the two women making love. I had my face up against the screen in awe. I thought, 'This makes so much sense!' Seeing this intimacy and fire caused me to burst inside. I felt all these feelings that I had repressed through the years come alive again. I was crying, watching the movie, because it was such an intense feeling."

Clair's faith had always been a "guiding light" in her life, so in the middle of her joy she turned to the Bible to understand more about her feelings. Reading Leviticus and other passages, she felt a new weight descend upon her. "I realized I couldn't talk to my pastor about it, or my friends at the Baptist church I was attending. I felt I would be too vulnerable if I talked to my church. They would condemn me. I was afraid about not being accepted. So I wound up isolating myself from them."

Clair began to lead a double life: "I'd go to church on Sunday and clubbing on Monday with my lesbian friends. But I lied to both groups. I was so divided. I couldn't share the joy of meeting a wonderful woman in my Christian community, and I couldn't talk about church in the lesbian community."

Feeling so at odds, "I felt I had to choose: be gay or be with God. I didn't want to choose." Clair took a trip to Europe. Prior to her departure, she prayed, "I would like this question answered: 'Can I reconcile being gay with being a Christian? Can I be both at the same time?'" Clair arrived in London and checked into a youth hostel. One of the first people she met was a woman named Virginia from Massachusetts. "I saw that she had rainbow earrings. I wondered if she was gay. We went out to breakfast and talked about our travel plans. I asked her why she decided to travel by herself. She said, 'It wasn't by choice. My girlfriend couldn't make it because she was pastoring a church and couldn't take the time off.' I jumped up and cried and cried and cried. I was so elated. I told her, 'This was my quest: to reconcile being gay and Christian. And the first person I meet on my trip is a lesbian Christian applying for seminary, with a pastor as a girlfriend!'" That night, Clair prayed, "Okay God, I hear it. I guess there is a place for me."[33]

Session Four

Scripture

The Bible is a treasure book
Of stories that are true...

— Children's Sunday school song

The Bible is a treasure book, filled with accounts of people and entire communities and countries living out a relationship with God. Sometimes these accounts reveal painful alienation from God and the consequences of living such a life. At other times, accounts of people seeking right relationship express the heart of humanity's deepest longing. While the stories are the records of communities that existed thousands of years ago, what they also offer to us is a living document, a place where our lives can intersect with the Word of God.

The "Good Book" is actually a collection of many books, written by many authors over a period of approximately fifteen hundred years. Mainly communicated orally, or painstakingly written by hand, the books were passed from one generation to the next. In 95 C.E., the first thirty-nine books of the canon (official books recognized as scripture) were selected to create what Christians call the Old Testament. In 397 C.E., church leaders meeting at the Council of Carthage identified what would become the twenty-seven books of the New Testament.

The original language of the books of the Old Testament was Hebrew, although they were later translated into Greek. The books of the New Testament used two languages — Greek and Aramaic. In 400 C.E., the entire Bible was translated into Latin. The Latin, or Vulgate (meaning "written in the language of the

74

people"), version would remain as the central text of Christianity until 1380 c.e., when the first English translation was begun. The King James Version was commissioned in 1611 c.e. This remained the primary English text of the Bible for more than three hundred years.

> Cantádmelas otra vez,
> Maravillosas palabras de vida.
>
> Sing them over again to me,
> Wonderful words of life!

One look at the religious section of your favorite bookstore will reveal that today we have many English translations and paraphrases of the Bible. Today, as in biblical times, people desire a relationship with God. To Christians seeking such a relationship, the text of the Bible is more than a historical document chronicling a long-ago people's search for God. It is a guidepost for contemporary seekers and continues to reveal the Word of God for our day.

As Christians, we place significant emphasis on the four Gospels: Matthew, Mark, Luke, and John. Because we are followers of Jesus Christ, his story becomes central to our story. We believe Jesus is the fulfillment of scripture, the long-awaited one, the Messiah, who has come to redeem a fallen humanity. As the Gospel of John describes, "And the Word became flesh and lived among us" (John 1:14). For Christians, Jesus Christ is the authentic Word of God. By truly encountering the Word of God who became flesh, died, and was resurrected, we are able to fully claim our identity as the sons and daughters of God.

The religious traditions of Jesus' era were a carefully detailed collection of rules and regulations, all with the intended purpose of helping people in their quest to be faithful to God. Jesus was frequently criticized for breaking the rules. Whether it was healing on the Sabbath or speaking to women or socializing with those considered unclean, Jesus showed how adherence to rules could prevent God's Word from breathing new life into others. He summed up the entire Hebraic law into two rules for living:

> You shall love the Lord your God with all your heart, and with all your soul, and with all your mind.... You shall love your neighbor as yourself. On these two commandments depend all the law and the prophets! (Matt. 22:37–40)

Jesus was doing something very radical. He emphasized the use of a love ethic in interpreting scripture and in our daily lives. As we move through this study reflecting on any statement, tradition, church rule, or legal rule, we invite you to constantly apply the simple test:

1. Does it allow all persons to love God?

2. When we choose to adhere to or support it, are we demonstrating a love for neighbor?

Sex and the Bible

When was the last time you heard a sermon about sex? Chances are, not in a long while, although there may be more preaching on this subject lately. What does the Bible say about sex? How has it affected our views on sex and sexuality?

Looking for sex in the Bible, one would find:

1. *Different roles and rules governing each gender.* A woman, for the most part, was considered property, not a person. Genesis 3:16 admonishes that the "husband shall rule over you." A woman had little legal rights or recourse, should she be mistreated. In fact, violence against women received little condemnation in the scriptures. Why is there so much focus on the intended mistreatment of Lot's visitors in Sodom (Gen. 19:5–7) while there is little attention given to the very next verse, when Lot offers to give his daughters over to the angry mob (Gen. 19:8)? How many of your Bible study classes ever included the story of the rape of the Levite's concubine (Judg. 19)?

Here, again, a woman and her body are offered in exchange for a man's safety.

While women were expected to remain virgins until marriage, this was not required of men (Deut. 22:13–21). Men's semen was considered the seed of life, while a woman's womb was just the incubator. To waste semen in any way not connected to procreation (like masturbation) was considered a violation of the natural order (Gen. 38:9).

The Holiness Codes, found in the book of Leviticus and written after the exile, were a way to distinguish the people of Israel — their lifestyle, their behavior, their religious practices — from those around them. Cleanliness was holiness. Bodily fluids connected to sexual and reproductive organs were seen as unclean (Lev. 12:1–8, 15). For women, this meant that she was unclean during menstruation, sexual intercourse, and childbirth. Men were considered unclean after ejaculation whether alone or during intercourse.

2. *Romantic love rarely mentioned.* Marriages were primarily arranged by parents and were a way to ensure the survival of both families. Sex was not related to romantic fulfillment, but to ensuring lineage. An exception is the Song of Solomon, which is an earthy expression of love between two persons.

3. *Sexual morality as a way to distinguish believers from nonbelievers.* Paul, seeking to strengthen the growing Jesus movement in a hostile culture, provides guidelines for living to help Christians deepen their own identity (Gal. 5:16–21). Note that while Jewish tradition frowned upon celibacy because of the importance of increasing the tribe of Israel, Paul placed high value on celibacy, viewing it as a way to focus one's entire being on God's work (1 Cor. 7). Likewise, Paul's condemnation of homosexual behavior is set in the context of idolatrous Roman practices (Rom. 1), which included the worship of idols and intercourse with both male and female sacred prostitutes. Paul had no understanding of homosexuality as an orientation.

He only understood it as a part of idolatrous practices that threatened the Jesus movement.

For many of us, these biblical messages about gender, romantic love, and sexual morality that we received about sex were communicated verbally and nonverbally. They are the underlying basis for such sayings as:

"Las buenas chicas se esperan hasta el matrimonio." (Good girls save it for marriage.)

"Mastúrbate y te saldrán pelos en las manos." (Masturbate and you'll grow hair on your hand.)

"Tú no está supuesta a disfrutarlo." (You're not supposed to enjoy it.)

"El sexo es algo sucio." (Sex is dirty.)

More Biblical Lessons

But are there other lessons about sex and human relationships found in the Bible? In reading the scriptures, several major themes emerge. For example:

1. *The extension of the definition of family.* Jesus makes it clear that kinship is no longer determined by economic arrangements or biology. Instead, family is created by faithful living. "Who are my mother and my brothers?" asks Jesus. "Whoever does the will of God is my brother, and sister, and mother" (Mark 3:31–35).

2. *Love underscores all relationships.* Jesus made it clear that our actions should be guided by love: love of God and neighbor. Paul places love as the highest virtue. For Paul, "love is patient; love is kind; love is not envious or boastful or arrogant or rude. . . . It bears all things, believes all things, hopes all things, endures all things." (1 Cor. 13:4–7)

Nowhere in the Bible are these themes found more vividly than in the Song of Solomon. Sensuous feeling, erotic love, and mutual pleasure between a man and a woman are celebrated. In this book, sexuality is seen as a delightful and good gift from God. Consider this excerpt:

> How beautiful you are, my love, how very beautiful! Your eyes are doves behind your veil. Your hair is like a flock of goats, moving down the slopes of Gilead. Your teeth are like a flock of shorn ewes that have come up from the washing, all of which bear twins, and not one among them is bereaved. Your lips are like a crimson thread, and your mouth is lovely. Your cheeks are like halves of a pomegranate behind your veil. Your neck is like the tower of David, built in courses; on it hang a thousand bucklers, all of them shields of warriors. Your two breasts are like two fawns, twins of a gazelle that feed among the lilies. (Song of Sol. 4:1–5)

What would our view of sex and sexuality be today if we were raised with more sermons and Sunday school lessons from the Song of Solomon?

Jannie, a white twelve-year-old girl, was at church camp. One night, Fritz the cook came out in his campfire talk, sharing with the campers his faith journey, which included coming to terms with his sexuality. The next morning, Jannie said to another camper: "My mother says that the Bible says that homosexuality is wrong, that homosexuals are evil, and God doesn't love them. But Fritz is so good to us, making sure we have yummy food for dinner and a great time at camp! I think my mother is wrong."

When discussing homosexuality, people often point to a couple of scripture passages and, without further study, say that homosexuality is not a part of God's plan for humankind. This kind of proof-texting fails to honor God and God's people. Truly encountering the Word of God in the Bible requires us to read it in community with others whose interpretations may challenge and inform our own.

GATHERING

Welcome one another to the group and begin to prepare for your time together.

Opening Scripture, Prayer, and Song

Read Matthew 22:36–40.

Pray together:

> Gracious God, author of the wonderful words of life, may we be open to your presence as we study the scriptures and discern your movement in our world and lives. We pray this in the name of Jesus, who was and is the Word made flesh. Amen.

Sing a song from your community's hymn or song book that talks about scripture (for example: "Wonderful Words of Life," "Thy Word," "I Love to Tell the Story").

If there is time, you may choose to review the assignments completed for this session (see page 69). How did you feel doing the experience project? Was it easy or hard for you? What did you learn about the way homosexuality is (or is not) reported in the newspaper?

Exercise 1: What Does It Say? (Facilitator's Guide, page 142)

The group will attempt to solve a scripture puzzle. Each person will be given a piece of paper with a word written on it by the facilitator. When the words are placed in the correct order they will form a familiar scripture verse. Without speaking to one another or looking up the verse, line up the words in a way that makes sense to you. Afterward, discuss this task.

1. Have you put the scripture together correctly? (Check with the facilitator)
2. What made this exercise difficult or easy for you?
3. What clues did you use to figure out what the words might mean?
4. When you study the Bible, what resources do you use to open up the meaning of scripture?

INFORMING

Our early encounters with scripture leave a lasting impression on us. The following exercise will help you recall how the Bible was a part of your childhood home.

Exercise 2: The Family Bible (Facilitator's Guide, page 142)

Step One:

Draw a picture of how the Bible was used by your family.

Step Two:

Share your picture with others in the group.

Step Three:

In small groups, answer the following questions:

1. When you were growing up, what was the main way your family used the Bible and its teachings?
2. How was the Bible used in your home with respect to the role of women and men? Sexuality? Premarital sex? Masturbation? Menstruation? Homosexuality? Procreation?

Exercise 3: Reading the Bible with Our Hearts and Our Minds (Facilitator's Guide, page 142)

Some of us were taught to recite Bible verses from memory. The assumption was that if we had the verse committed to memory, it would inform how we live. As adults, we know that it takes much more than memory for the scriptures to come alive for us. It requires the involvement of our hearts *and* our minds. When we read the Bible, we are at the same time reaching back to understand a long-ago, faraway people and asking ourselves what truth emerges for us and our time. Using reason, we are able to see how God's Word continues to speak to us in our human condition.

Biblical scholars help us understand a world very different from our own. They set the scriptures in their cultural contexts. They teach us how the verses were edited and compiled in differing historical periods. They help us be aware of the faith traditions from which the scriptures emerged. When we study biblical passages through the lens of biblical scholarship, meanings and understandings emerge that we might otherwise overlook.

Discuss in small groups:

1. How were you trained to read and understand the Bible?

2. What tools and resources do you use to understand the context of a Bible passage?

3. Can you give an example of how your understanding of a Bible passage changed when you utilized both the tools and resources of biblical scholarship and your personal insights?

Whenever we read the Bible, it is through the lens of the tradition in which we've been raised and our own personal encounter with scripture. Hear these different voices and their approaches to scripture:

I was told that the Bible was infallible. When I asked how come some things were contradicted in Scripture, I was told I was not respecting God's Word. It left me very conflicted about Scripture and belief. — forty-six-year-old white woman

The Word had always been important to me. I had such a desire for God and being in God's Word. When I found a queer Asian group that took the Bible seriously, I finally felt my two halves, lesbian and Christian, come together. — thirty-two-year-old Asian woman

If we accepted homosexuality, it would mean the Bible was wrong, and it would cease to be God's Word. — fifty-two-year-old black man

I don't remember much Bible study when I was a child. But I do remember being told over and over that God loves me. Reading the Bible as an adult, I see it through these eyes: God loves me, and has something important to tell me. — forty-five-year-old white woman

Discussion questions:

1. What messages did your faith community give you about the Bible? How was it seen as a resource of faith?
2. How have those messages about the Bible from your past informed how you have lived?
3. How were questions about the Bible treated?
4. If you were to tell a young person why the Bible should be important to them, what would you say?
5. According to the Bible, is sexuality a gift from God? Where do you see your opinion reflected in scripture?

FOCUSING

Exercise 4: Yada, Yada, Yada... (Facilitator's Guide, page 143)

When talking about homosexuality, seldom is the whole Bible, or even Jesus' summary of Hebraic law (Matt. 22:37–40), taken into account. Instead, there is a focus on seven (7!) texts, only some of which refer to same-sex behavior. Let's look at one of the scriptures used to denounce homosexuality and use our tool of reason to try to understand it.

Step One:

Break into two groups and follow the directions for your group.

Group one: Read Genesis 19:1–19. Answer the following questions:

1. What did the men of Sodom want of the angelic visitors?
2. Why did Lot offer them his daughters?
3. Why was Sodom destroyed?
4. When was it decided that Sodom would be destroyed?
5. What does this scripture have to do with homosexuality?

Group two: Read Genesis 19:1–19. Before answering questions, read the following to see what other writers had to say about Sodom: Deuteronomy 29:22–23, Isaiah 1:9–17, Ezekiel 16:46–50, Luke 10:8–12, and 2 Peter 2:4–10. Answer the following questions:

1. What did the men of Sodom want of the angelic visitors?
2. Why did Lot offer them his daughters?
3. Why was Sodom destroyed?
4. When was it decided that Sodom would be destroyed?
5. How do the other scriptures help in understanding Genesis 19?
6. What does Genesis 19 have to do with homosexuality?

Step Two:

Come together and share your responses.

The story of the destruction of Sodom and Gomorrah has been interpreted as God's condemnation of homosexuality. In fact, the word "sodomy" is derived from this city. In the past, sodomy has been understood as any form of nonprocreative sexual act, including masturbation and oral and anal sex. Sodomy was considered a sin, but in 1533 sodomy became a crime when King Henry VIII of England adopted church doctrine into a system of laws as a way to break from the Roman Catholic Church.

In June 2003, the U.S. Supreme Court struck down states' sodomy laws. These legal statutes covered a wide range of sexual behavior, but are best known for prohibiting oral and anal sex, even between consenting adults. Most sodomy laws applied both to heterosexuals and homosexuals. However, they were mainly enforced against homosexuals.

> Many contemporary exegetes agree that the Old Testament story about the destruction of Sodom cannot be read as a lesson about divine punishment of same-sex copulation. If any lesson is wanted from the story, the lesson would seem to be about hospitality.
> — Mark Jordan, white church history professor[34]

Bible readers have equated Sodom with homosexual behavior because of *yada*, the verb "to know," which is used in Genesis 19:5: "Bring the men out that we may know (*yada*) them." *Yada* appears in the Hebrew scriptures 943 times. It is used to know God, truth, the law, people, places, and good and evil. Here, in Genesis 19, is the only time it has been translated to denote a sexual knowing.

The connection between Sodom and homosexuality is a cultural creation, rooted in the same culture that never wonders about the implications of Lot's offer of his daughters to the crowd. Why do we skip over this section of the story and instead focus on the desire of the crowd to "know" the angelic visitors? We ignore the violence against women and inhospitality.

Step Three:

Discussion questions:

1. What questions do you still have about this text?
2. Why do you think people focus on Sodom's sin as homosexuality rather than inhospitality?
3. What has this exercise taught you about reading the Bible?

Exercise 5: Body Charades (Facilitator's Guide, page 143)

Throughout this study, we have been exploring ways to celebrate an embodied theology that celebrates sexuality as a good
gift from God. This exercise is a way for us to use our bodies to
communicate in fun ways.

Pick someone to go first. The facilitator will whisper a word
that the person must spell out to the group, using his or her body,
no words or symbols.

> What is revealing about all this is that nowhere in
> the Old or New Testaments is the sin of Sodom,
> the cause of its sudden and terrible destruction,
> equated with homosexuals or with homosexuality.
> The attempted homosexual rape of the angels at
> Lot's door, while vivid and distasteful, is hardly the
> subject of the story or the cause of the punishment,
> and no one in scripture suggests that it was.
>
> — *Peter Gomes, African American,*
> *Harvard Divinity School faculty*[35]

TAKING NOTE

In your journal, answer the following questions:

1. When do you consult the Bible for your own sexual practices?

2. When do you consult the Bible about others' sexual practices?

3. What would a healthy biblically informed sense of one's own
   sexuality consist of for:

   - an elderly single person living in assisted living?
   - a college student?
   - a developmentally challenged person?

Assignments for Next Session

1. Read the introduction to the next session (page 88).

2. Watch the video *The Big Eden*, the story of a gay New York artist who returns to Montana to be with his dying grandfather.

3. Keep a record of one thing that you do each day because it is a (family, social, church, or ethnic) tradition to do it.

Closing Prayer

Sex is a good gift from God! Pass a lit candle around the circle. When the candle is passed to you, offer a prayer, aloud or silent, of what you are thankful for about sex.

Going Deeper: The Song of Solomon

Step One:
Read aloud the Song of Solomon.

Step Two:
Popcorn the images you heard. No censoring!

Step Three:
How did the lovers feel about each other?

Step Four:
How would you describe the theology of sexuality that is found here?

Step Five:
How can the Song of Solomon be used by the church to instruct about sex and sexuality?

Session Five

Sex and Tradition

From the time I turned eighteen and left for college, I was anxious to be independent and only returned home for brief visits with my Mom. This is when the "birthday call" tradition began. My Mom started calling me every year on my birthday at the exact time that she gave birth to me (4:16 am). I remember how annoying I found this tradition to be, though I would never tell her that. When she called me she would always say, "Hello darling. This is the exact moment when a special miracle came into my life . . . years ago. You, darling. I can remember hearing the doctor tell me, 'look up, look up, look at your baby.' At that moment I started thanking the Lord for this amazing blessing of bringing you into my life and I have never stopped thanking Him for blessing me with you. Happy Birthday, my sweet baby girl." When she said this, I would sleepily grunt, "Thanks, Mom." After I put the telephone receiver down and began trying to get back to sleep, I would irritably mutter to myself, "Why couldn't she wait and tell me all of that stuff in five or six hours?" Now I am a middle-aged woman and my Mom has been dead for about ten years. I miss her terribly. Oh, how I long for another chance to hear her loving voice at 4:16 a.m. on my birthday. . . .

Tradition is a single habit or a collection of certain habits that are a regular part of our lives. Whether or not we are aware of it, there are many traditions that we incorporate into our everyday behavior, such as eating turkey on Thanksgiving, saying "thank you" and "please" to someone who is helping you, wearing a bra if you are a woman or a male-to-female transgender person, or making sure that the body of a loved one who has died is buried or cremated. We may not know who originally thought of these traditional ways of behaving, but we think of them as what you are "supposed to do." If we were to spend time investigating them, often we would find multiple explanations for why the traditions in our civic, family, and religious lives are significant.

> "¿Qué es un bisexual?" my mother asked when I came out to her. I told her that I am attracted to members of both sexes and have the ability to fall in love with both....I educate people in my peer group, in my academic community, and in my cultural community. It just never stops. Now when people ask, "¿Qué es un bisexual?" I smile and proudly answer "Yo soy!"
>
> — *Obie Leyva, Latino (Chicano) bisexual,*
> *Berkeley, California*[36]

Tradition gives our lives a sense of order. But do we maintain tradition because we are simply following the traditional ways of behaving perpetuated by the dominant majority of our society? Or is tradition something we have deliberately chosen to maintain because it contributes something positive and valuable to our lives?

When the author of a novel describes the characters in the book, did you ever notice how you assume that the characters are white without being told that they are? The traditional style of writing novels is for the author not to mention the racial/ethnic background of the characters unless they are Latino/Hispanic, Asian/Asian American, Native American, or African American. If the author does not specify a racial/ethnic background, you are to assume that the characters are "just normal people," which, in this society, usually refers to white people. Why do we hold onto this way of privileging white people in the traditional style of writing for every novel and short story that gets published?

Tradition in Local Church Life

In our local churches, it is also not clear whether tradition is formed by habit or because the whole community desires it and has intentionally agreed to it.

Consider the location of the choir during Sunday morning worship. When the choir sings their anthem, if they remain seated in their designated pews in the front of the sanctuary, someone in the church might refer to that practice by saying, "That's the

> The first in my family to go to college, how did I become a professor in a five-college system at a major University? Reared in racism, prone to violence, and steeped in religion, how did I join a scholarly world dedicated to humane values and freedom of ideas? Immersed in an extended family of more cousins than I could count, what prepared me to read and write and study alone among Yankees of whom I had always been suspicious? Most of all, how did the dark secret of being different, of crossing sexualities and loyalties and sin and salvation, shape my life? On this snowy morning in New England, with a Confederate flag on my desk, how did I come to be half a century, two thousand miles, and 40 degrees from home? ... We grow up with a powerful sense of place, living on the land with fierce loyalties to family. So this is my story, telling it the best I can about my life as a southerner and a lesbian.
>
> — Bonnie R. Strickland, white lesbian,
> raised in Birmingham, Alabama[37]

traditional way things are supposed to be." That same person might even attach a theological reason to this tradition, like, "It's important for members of the congregation to always have the cross as their focus during worship since as Christians, the cross is at the center of our faith. If the entire choir got out of their seats and stood in front of the congregation, it would distract from the cross and make it impossible for the congregation to be able to maintain their proper focus."

Should this local church custom be considered part of the Christian tradition? For some people, in order for it to be part

---

That year [at age eighteen], I began attending a Christian church while in school and hung out with a Christian crowd. There were no other Natives in this group.... Well we all got down on our knees and they prayed that this spirit of homosexuality would leave me. It wasn't until years later when I sat with that Medawin elder that I realized that if what she had said was true, then if the spirit of homosexuality left me then my own spirit would too, for they were inexplicably intertwined. [But, while still in the Christian group,] I prayed that God would take the spirit of homosexuality from me. Then I had prayed, fasted, and cried some more. I just wanted to die. It took me a couple of years before I saw the light and decided to leave. I heard about a group of Queer Natives from all over North America who were getting together. They were learning ceremonies and teaching them to each other.... I learned that Natives had historically honored the path that the Creator had made for Two-Spirit people.

— *Raven E. Heavy Runner, Native American gay man*[38]

of the Christian tradition, it would be important for the entire
congregation (at least) to consider this practice and the reasons for
it, and then to have collectively agreed to it. In other words, the
opinion of one individual Christian does not constitute Christian
tradition. On the other hand, why doesn't a thoughtful viewpoint by a church member, which is based on his or her Christian
theological beliefs, constitute Christian tradition?

> [In the sixteenth and seventeenth centuries,]
> missionaries throughout Latin America preached
> that God had sent the Spanish to conquer the
> Indians because they had engaged in sodomitical
> behavior, and . . . confessionals advised priests to ask
> their parishioners about sodomitical behavior, both
> homosexual and heterosexual. Pérez Bocanegra's
> extensive penitential [1631, Andes] includes
> questions for men asking if they had touched or
> been touched by male friends, and for women
> asking whether they had "sinned with another
> woman, like yourself"? . . . Special prayers for
> delivery from sodomy were printed in Mexico City
> in the early eighteenth century.[39]

We all bring our own understandings of Christian tradition into
the church, and those understandings should be treated respectfully. But who has the authority to create Christian tradition? Is
one person sufficient? Or one congregation? Do you "win" the authority to do so if you have the most people on your side? When
we differ with one another about tradition, who should have the
authority to declare which ideas are authentic parts of Christianity
and which ideas are heresy?

How do we stay open to the revelation of God's will? These are
not new questions for Christians. The process of creating Christian tradition has occurred over many centuries through both the

written words and organized actions of many people in differing parts of the world.

Church History as Tradition

Christianity has an enormous legacy of tradition. In the first century, Christian tradition was one small aspect of Jewish tradition. As this Jewish-Christian movement spread to differing towns and cities, tradition evolved through the varying practices of the evangelists and the stories they told about Jesus and his followers. These stories spread through accounts that were eventually included in the official canon of the Bible, like the Gospel of Mark and the Luke-Acts stories. Evangelists also taught about Jesus through accounts that were later excluded from the Bible, like the Gospel of Mary Magdalene and the Gospel of Thomas. After the Emperor Constantine recognized Christianity as an official religion in the Roman Empire (386 C.E.), Christian tradition continued to spread and grow at a more rapid pace in the ancient Mediterranean and North African world. Among ancient Christians, traditions concerned with institutionalizing the church increased and were added to the traditions of the early church movement previously persecuted by the Roman state. Centuries later, medieval European church traditions, which included monastic life as well as crusades killing Muslims and Jews, multiplied. At the same time, more entrenched organizational traditions continued to grow in Jerusalem and Rome. Many variations of Christian tradition grew out of the European Protestant Reformation movement in the 1500s and evolved through Christianity's role in the African slave trade.

From about the sixteenth and seventeenth centuries onward, Christian tradition in the Americas again encompassed diverse forms, with a range including Puritan, Quaker, and Catholic beliefs. Here the major currents of Christian tradition encompassed justifications for the rape and genocide of indigenous Native peoples together with the theft of their land, as well as for the system of chattel slavery for African Americans. It also included conflicts about baptism, witchcraft, and the disposition of the soul after death. Throughout the nineteenth and early twentieth centuries certain understandings of Christian tradition were launched from the United States through missionary movements among people in Asia and Africa. Christian tradition evolved through interactions with the varied cultural traditions that the missionaries encountered in each context.

Today Christian tradition is defined by Catholic and Orthodox church doctrine, as well as by the doctrine and polity of hundreds of Protestant denominations and independent church organizations throughout the world. It is expressed in the behavior of millions of ordinary Christians worldwide who give witness to the Christian faith tradition in their daily lives.

> My mom wasn't accepting of my sexuality because she's extremely religious. . . . My father, I thought that he would be the one who would act the way my mother did, but um, he was supportive from the beginning. I told him and he said, like, "You're my son, I love you. I don't care."
>
> *— Quincy Greene, twenty-year-old Caribbean American (born in Guyana), who lives in Philadelphia*[40]

For Jesus, tradition was something he came to fulfill through his mission and ministry. When starting out, Jesus announced to his own Jewish faith community that the prophetic scriptural tradition about God's promise to send someone to liberate the oppressed was fulfilled on that day (Luke 4:16–22). Tradition was also something that he came to reinterpret. Jesus rebuked religious leaders for being concerned about how his disciples broke with tradition, saying to them: "For the sake of tradition, you make void the word of God. You hypocrites! Isaiah prophesied rightly about you when he said: 'This people honors me with their lips, but their hearts are far from me; in vain do they worship me, teaching human precepts as doctrines' " (Matt. 15:6–9). The religious authorities persecuted Jesus for behavior that violated the official understandings of tradition. After he violated tradition by healing the man with the withered hand on the Sabbath, the leaders "immediately" conspired against him in order to figure out how "to destroy him" (Mark 3:6).

"¿Cuál es el significado de la palabra tradición para ti?" (What is the meaning of tradition for you?) This session examines a small sampling of Christian historical sources concerned with our faith and sexuality. As we have done in previous sessions, we focus on the role of reason in our theology, asking: How do we use reason to interpret ideas about faith and sexuality that are found in Christian tradition? How do we choose the most important parts of the Christian tradition to be passed on to the next generation of Christians?

GATHERING

Opening Scripture, Prayer, and Song

The scripture reading is from the beginning of the book of Job, after Job has been afflicted by the death of his children, his servants, and the theft of his livestock; Job offers an anguished prayer filled with questions for God.

- Read Job 7:17–20.

- Sing a song about tradition from your community's hymn or song book, for example: "Faith of the Ages" ("Faith of Our Fathers").

Question Prayer

Often when we pray we ask God questions. Asking God questions is a way of opening ourselves up for God's guidance and support. Because God is our friend, accompanying us throughout our life's journey, it's okay to ask God about anything.

Praying about sexuality may be something that you have already done by yourself or with your sexual partner. This is an opportunity to lift up your questions about what it means as a church group to discuss sexuality and Christianity. By focusing on our questions for God, we are part of a long tradition of faithful Christian people who have sought to express their ideas about God by being in dialogue with one another. Also, when we offer our questions to God in prayer, we practice the spiritual discipline of prayer, emphasizing the use of our reason.

Step One:

Write down one question you have for God. Below are examples to help get you started.

- Loving God, I feel your presence in this room as we gather to talk about sexuality, will you guide our conversations about . . . ?
- Holy God, as we think together about your gift of sexuality to us, how do I know whether or not . . . ?

Step Two:

Close with the following prayer.

> With humility, sincerity, and openness, we lift up our questions to you O God, in the name of Jesus Christ we pray. Amen.

Let's gather our thoughts on tradition by considering its broader meaning for our lives and families. Tradition is part of our personal story! Below is a series of questions to stimulate your thinking.

Exercise 1: Make a Tradition Platter (Facilitator's Guide, page 145)

Each person creates a "tradition platter" by adding items to their plate during the three steps of this exercise.

Step One: Family Food Traditions

Family food traditions consist of the actual food dishes that your family prepares as well as the rituals of gathering, cooking, offering a blessing, eating, and cleaning up that surround those food traditions. In general, what family food traditions have been important in your own life? Have any of them been "passed down" from one generation to another in your family, ethnic group, or the region of the country where you were raised?

Examples: There may be traditional foods that you like. Maybe there is a favorite dish you love to eat or prepare. Your family may have a tradition where all of the women do the cooking, serving, and cleaning up while the men sit down and enjoy the meal. Or there may be a blessing you always invoke together.

Make clay objects that represent those food traditions in your family and put them on your platter. They can be literal representations or symbolic ones.

Step Two: Spoken Sexuality Traditions

What messages about sex were "passed down" to you by your family members and community, for example, parents, siblings, older cousins, friends at school? When you were growing up, what was said directly about sexuality in your family or by your friends in the neighborhood, perhaps in relation to movies or television programs, about the size or dimensions of girls' hips or boys' penises, rules about using tampons, or sexual jokes?

Write the message down on a file card and add it to your platter.

Step Three: Unspoken Traditions

What nonverbal messages did you receive about sexuality? For example: a secret about childhood sexual abuse; attitudes you learned through words you were not allowed to say — like euphemisms for penis, vagina, menstruation; a gay relative who was rarely mentioned or whose sexual orientation was kept a secret?

Cut out a circle with a hole in the middle to represent the silence. If it was a big secret, make a bigger circle with a hole in the middle. Write the message that you learned on the border of the circle. Add your circle to your platter.

Step Four: Explain!

Choose one item from your platter and tell the story of what it means and why you put it on your platter.

Going Deeper

Our "tradition platter" includes items we did not choose to make a part of our lives. Sometimes it includes items we would not have chosen. There may also be traditions we'd like to add. We wish that certain rituals and spoken and unspoken messages had been present to nurture us in ways that we needed during our personal journey to adulthood.

Imagine you have the power to select and create family food rituals and sexuality messages that would contribute to a positive sense of family and sexuality. Then, take a look at your tradition platter and imagine one item you would like to add or one item you'd like to remove. If you are comfortable doing so, share what you have chosen and why.

INFORMING

- Who said?
- Who said What?
- Who said What about *sex?*
- Who said What about *sex* in Christian Tradition?

Exercise 2: "Who Said What?" Skit (Facilitator's Guide, page 145)

Many of us are not aware of the ways Christian tradition has impacted our understandings about sex, sexuality, and gender. This skit is a brief tour of a few major Christian theologians and their thoughts on these topics.

Assign members of your group the following parts, and then read the play aloud.

Tour Guide	Hildegard of Bingen
Questioner	Twelfth-century Monastic Brother
Augustine	Martin Luther
Aquinas	John Calvin
Julian of Norwich	John Wesley

Tour Guide: Welcome to the Christian tradition tour. We'll be focusing on discussions of sexuality from the Christian tradition, but you also get a bonus discussion on gender. The theologians we'll hear from will speak on sexuality and how the two opposite sexes of humanity are linked in Christian —

Questioner: Wait! I don't get it? Since today we no longer refer to the idea that there are just two sexes, are you saying that for the theo —

Tour Guide: That's nonsense. There are two, opposite sexes. Let's go on.

Questioner: I'm trying to ask you about what these theologians will discuss. Will it be the sexist tradition of making rigid rules for two *genders*, like, that males are strong, tough, decisive, dominant, and that females are tender, fragile, caring, and submissive?

Tour Guide: Tradition, that's what we're here for. Now let's hear from . . .

Questioner: Hey, wait a sec, answer my question! Do they discuss gender like there are two opposite genders? Because, that's wrong. There are really several sex/gender categories for people that include combinations of personality and biological traits. Like there are people with only male sexual organs, people with only female sexual organs, and people who have both male and female biological traits and organs. And biology isn't linked to specific personality traits!

Tour Guide: You're confusing me and delaying the tour. Ah, look, here we are at our first stop. Be quiet and listen to the founders of our Christian theological tradition.

Augustine: I am Bishop Augustine of Hippo, an African bishop who wrote during the fourth century. When I interpret Paul's view in 1 Corinthians 11:7 in my work *The Trinity*, I explain that "...separately in her quality as a helpmeet, which regards the woman alone, then she is not the image of God, but, as regards the man alone, he is the image of God as fully and completely as when the woman too is joined with him in one."[41]

Questioner: Do women have value in God's sight, apart from when they are having sex with men?

Augustine: I also explain "the sense of shame in sexual inter-course." The "evil of lust, specifically in its sexual meaning" must be understood. There are lusts for many things, like vengeance or money. But, "...when lust is mentioned without specification of its object the only thing that normally occurs to the mind is the lust that excites the indecent parts of the body. This lust assumes power not only over the whole body—"[42]

Questioner: Why are you so interested in how people get sexually excited? (giggles)

Tour Guide: Shhhh! Be respectful when you talk to the church fathers.

Augustine: Yes, keep quiet. I'm the bishop, and I haven't finished instructing you. "It is worse to lie with one's mother, than with the wife of another. But worse than all of these is what is done against nature, as when a man would want to use a woman's member not given for this.... Now the natural use if done beyond measure is something venial with a wife, something damnable with a prostitute. What is against nature is execrable if done with a prostitute, but more execrable if done with a wife—"[43]

Questioner: Well, I don't know what "execrable" means, but I think I still get the point. This is just the same thing we all say, about how guys have to marry a good girl, but shouldn't try the really fun sex stuff with her because she's a good girl. For that, they should go out and fool around with a... [Augustine exits.]

Tour Guide: Shut up! Please continue Bishop. Bishop? Bishop? Oh, no. He's gone. I hope he wasn't insulted by your unimportant questions.

Questioner: But if I don't ask questions, how will I ever understand these guys? I'm here to understand the Christian tradition, right? Aren't I allowed to use my own powers of reason to sort out the ideas so I can —

Tour Guide: Be patient and listen. Things will become clearer to you. Let's move on to Father Aquinas.

Aquinas: I am Thomas Aquinas, born in 1225. In my great work, *Summa Theologica,* I wrote that: "... among perfect animals the active power of generation belongs to the male sex, and the passive power to the female.... As regards the individual nature, woman is defective and misbegotten, for the active force in the male seed tends to the production of a perfect likeness in the masculine sex.... For good order would have been wanting in the human family if some were not governed by others wiser than themselves. So by such a kind of subjection woman is naturally subject to man, because in man the discretion of reason predominates."[44]

Questioner: Is this what I'm supposed to believe about women and their sexuality? That they're defective creatures, unable to think wisely because they don't produce semen, and naturally subordinate to men?! These ideas are repeated over and over again in the Christian tradition. Is this what *God* wants me to believe about women? Aren't there any women theologians in the Christian tradition?

Julian: I'm a woman! I'm Julian of Norwich, England. I was born in 1342.

Tour Guide: She's considered a medieval mystic, not a theologian.

Questioner: Why? Because she's a woman? That's just a sexist way of discounting her theology! What were her ideas, anyway?

Julian: Based on my visions from God, I proclaimed that in the making of humanity, "God is our kindly Father and God all-wisdom is our kindly Mother, with love and goodness of the Holy Spirit, which is all one God, one Lord.... I saw that the second person who is our Mother substantially, the same dear person who is now become our Mother sensually. For of God's making we are double; that is to say, substantial and sensual."[45]

Questioner: Are you saying *sensuality* is good? Please, I want someone in "the" Christian tradition to say something good about human sensuality!

Julian: "Our substance is that higher part which we have of our Father God Almighty. And the second person of the Trinity is our Mother in kind, in our substantial making — in whom we are grounded and rooted; and he is our Mother of mercy in taking our sensuality.... As truly as God is our Father, so truly is God our Mother."[46]

Questioner: I knew it! I knew it! I knew that the women would be different! I knew that a woman theologian would say something affirming about humanity and sensuality, and about how to understand God. Are any other women's ideas allowed in Christian tradition?

Hildegard: I'm Hildegard of Bingen, powerful abbess of two monasteries for nuns in Germany during the eleventh century. In my visions from God, God spoke to me saying, "Those of female sex should not approach the office of my altar; for they are infirm and [of] weak habitation, appointed to bear children and diligently nurture them...."[47]

Questioner: Wait...why are you saying such restrictive things about women?

Hildegard: In addition, "A man who sins with another man as if with a woman sins bitterly against God and against the union with which God united male and female. Hence both in God's sight are polluted, black and wanton, horrible and harmful to God and humanity....."[48]

Questioner: Okay, okay, I get the point. So is heterosexual sex good?

Hildegard: "And a man who sins with a woman by this same method of perverted fornication is a voracious wolf of wickedness...and these are in my sight equally unworthy and unclean since they forsake the proper way of uniting with a woman...."[49]

Questioner: So what's the proper way for men and women to have sex?

Hildegard: Don't pretend that you don't know what's right. Furthermore, "Men who touch their own genital organ and emit their semen seriously imperil their souls, for they excite themselves to distraction; they appear to Me as impure animals devouring their own whelps, for they wickedly produce their semen only for abusive pollution. And women who imitate them in this unchaste touching, and excite themselves to bodily convulsions by providing their burning lust, are extremely guilty, for they pollute themselves with uncleanness when they should be keeping themselves in chastity."[50]

Questioner: Mother Hildegard, those nuns and priests must have been masturbating a lot for you to write so much about it, right? But how did you know? Same-sex relationships among priests must have existed or you wouldn't have offered those strong condemnations of their behavior, right?

Tour Guide: In some Christian communities same-sex love was not only accepted, but idealized. A ceremony for Holy Unions between priests was used in some medieval church traditions. Listen to a fragment of the ceremony that has been preserved.

Twelfth-century Monastic Brother chants: "O Lord our God, dwelling in heaven but looking down on that which is below, you who for the salvation of the human race sent your only begotten son, Jesus, and took Peter and Paul and made them brothers by consecration, make also these your servants (Name of person) and (Name of person) like those two apostles. Keep them blameless all the days of their lives . . . consider as worthy of union these two, joined not by nature but by the holy spirit of fidelity and unity of mind, just as you united Serge and Bacchus, Cosmas and Damian. . . ."[51]

Questioner: Where are the ideas of priests who joined in those medieval holy unions? Why don't we have their theological views highlighted in Christian tradition?

Tour Guide: I don't have time to answer your questions. The tour is almost over and —

Questioner: How could this tour be almost over? Are we only going to hear from Europeans? What about African Christians? Korean Christians? Filipino Christians? Aren't they part of "the" Christian tradition? Don't their theological views count? Doesn't omitting them only reinforce a racist belief in the intellectual superiority of Europeans that is already so common?

Tour Guide: Let me now present Martin Luther, the person who initiated the Protestant reformation in Germany during the sixteenth century.

Luther: I'm Martin Luther. Remember that " . . . if the woman had not been deceived by the serpent and had not sinned, she would have been the equal of Adam in all respects. For the punishment, that she is now subjected to the man, was imposed on her after sin and because of sin, just as the other hardships and dangers were: travail, pain, and countless other vexations. Therefore Eve was not like the woman of today; her state was far better and more excellent, and she was in no respect inferior to Adam."[52]

Questioner: Why does everything have to go back to how we interpret that Adam and Eve story?

Luther: I also have strong views on marriage, divorce, and sexuality. "Thus it is on the grounds of adultery one person may leave the other . . . it is praiseworthy to divorce an adulterous wife. . . . The same principle applies in the case of a wife with an adulterous husband. ... But a public divorce, whereby one [innocent party] is enabled to remarry, must take place through the investigation of a civil authority so that the adultery may be manifest to all. ... "[53]

Tour Guide: For those unfamiliar with the tradition, Luther was a Catholic priest, and this is a major departure from the Catholic Church's position opposing divorce.

Luther: Don't think that I've forgotten about the adulterer. "You may ask, 'What is to become of the other [guilty party] if he too is perhaps unable to lead a chaste life?' It was a reason that God commanded in the law [Deut. 22:22–24] that adulterers be stoned, that they might not have to answer this question. The temporal sword and government should therefore still put adulterers to death, for whoever commits adultery has in fact already departed and is considered as one dead."[54]

Questioner: Wow! That's a tough way to treat people who have extramarital affairs! Why do some Christians support rules about excluding gays and lesbians because Christian tradition says so, but don't also advocate the execution of heterosexual married men and women who have extramarital sexual affairs, since tradition says we should do that too? Why is it that only certain parts of the tradition matter?

Tour Guide: This tour teaches that the Christian tradition values what's right, not what's wrong! Keep listening and all your questions will be answered.

John Calvin: I am John Calvin, and in the sixteenth century I wrote, "Let every man abstain from marriage only so long as he is fit to observe celibacy. If his power to tame lust fails him, let him recognize that the Lord has now imposed the necessity of marriage upon him."[55]

Questioner: You're not a very romantic fellow, are you, Reverend Calvin? Shouldn't people get married, not because of a man's uncontrollable sex drive, but because *both* people love and respect each other and want to be lifelong partners?

John Wesley: I'm John Wesley. Writing in the eighteenth century, I affirmed the importance of marriage but "upon the whole, without disputing whether the married or single life be the more perfect state ... we may safely say, Blessed are 'they who have made themselves eunuchs for the kingdom of heaven's sake.' ... "[56] And for those who are blessedly celibate and single, they must not engage in masturbation because it causes symptoms in men such as weakness, effeminacy, paralysis, and the most painful of all gouts.[57]

Questioner: Wow, Reverend Wesley, what exactly were men doing when they masturbated to get such awful —

Tour Guide: We're out of time. Everybody take a bow so we can get ready for the next tour.

All (except Questioner): God's grace and peace be with you. Goodbye. (Bow)

> How open our own church should be to revising old and honored traditions continues to be a matter of debate.   *— Presbyterian Minority Report 1991*[58]

FOCUSING

Let's reach for our tool of reason. Reason helps us to sort out what we think about the tradition we've just heard about in the skit.

Exercise 3: Feelings Matter (Facilitator's Guide, page 146)

Let's not fall into that old trap of separating our process of thinking from what we are feeling. Let's employ our ability to reason by sorting out our feelings. How do you feel about that sampling of Christian theological tradition that we just heard?

Reflect on your feelings by completing the following sentences on the posted newsprint.

- I feel disappointed when I hear . . .
- I feel inspired when I hear . . .
- I feel that I need to know more about . . .
- I was shocked to hear . . .
- I feel that something should be added to this sampling of the tradition that mentions . . .

Exercise 4: Who Belongs at the Margin?
Who Belongs at the Center? (Facilitator's Guide, page 146)

Let's continue to focus on the Christian tradition in the skit. Based on some of those ideas, try to identify the parts of Christian tradition that you think should be passed on to the next generation of Christians and why it's important to do so.

Step One:

Decide what's in and what's out. Each person is given the following statements written on six color-coded pieces of poster board:

1. Celibacy/virginity is ideal Christian sexuality.
2. Women are subordinate to men because of Eve's sinfulness.
3. Homosexual sex is prohibited.
4. Masturbation is sinful.
5. The church should offer holy celebrations of same-sex unions.
6. Heterosexual sex is only for procreation, never for pleasure.

The facilitator will read the statements one at a time. As each one is read aloud, participants take out the card with the matching statement on it, and place it in the room according to how central or marginal to the Christian tradition the participant feels the statement should be. Areas of the room will be marked off with labels designating:

- *Central* traditions of Christianity that you believe should be passed on to the next generation of Christians to believe and uphold.

- *Marginal* traditions of Christianity that should be treated as less important for future generations to believe and uphold.

- Traditions of Christianity that should be *rejected*, perhaps atoned for, but not passed on as a tradition to be upheld by future generations of Christians.

Step Two:

Reflect on your choices. After all six of the statements are read and the cards placed throughout the room, go around the room and review the placement of the cards.

Gather and briefly discuss the choices that have been made by comparing the similarities and differences in the placement of the statements around the room. Think about whether your choices differ from the ones that were passed down to you. Which ones were taught to you as central and which ones were taught as marginal to the tradition?

Step Three:

Explain the reasons for your choices. What are the specific criteria that you used when making at least *one* of your choices about why something should be passed on as central, marginal, or rejected? As you list your criteria, consider how individual and community relationships with God are nurtured or eroded by this aspect of Christian tradition. You may want to use the following format to describe the criteria for your choices.

- *Central:* The next generation of Christians should be taught that _____ in Christian tradition is of central importance for guiding our faith and actions because . . .

- *Marginal:* The next generation of Christians should be taught that _____ in Christian tradition is of marginal importance for guiding our faith and actions because . . . .

- *Rejected:* The next generation of Christians should be taught that _____ in Christian tradition must be rejected as a guide for our faith and actions because . . .

Think about whose perspective informs your decision making about what is central in the Christian tradition and what is not. Think about what difference it makes:

- if you are a thirty-year-old white gay man seeking a partner to share your Christian faith and life (including a mutual, monogamous sexual relationship)?
- if you are a married, fifty-year-old, Latino heterosexual who enjoys a playful, mutually pleasuring sexual relationship?
- if you are an eighty-five-year-old widow and masturbation in the privacy of your bedroom is your only sexual outlet, and one of the only times you feel like a healthy, whole woman rather than a dependent child or a burden?

Going Deeper: The Church and Tradition

What is your theology of the church in relation to tradition?

Which of the following statements comes closest to your own primary theological understanding of the role of the church? Create a pantomime (with others in your group who selected the same statement) illustrating what it means.

1. The church is called by God to conserve Christian tradition concerning sexuality.
2. The church is called by God to interpret Christian tradition concerning sexuality in ways that build up Christian faith in the present.
3. The church is called by God to create Christian tradition concerning sexuality in an ongoing response to God's continuing revelations for each new generation of Christians.

Going Deeper: What's Healthy?

Step One:

Divide into two groups and have each group collect ideas about what's healthy and unhealthy in the sampling of Christian perspectives offered in the skit.

Spirituality Group: Which ideas about gender and sexuality help to build healthy spirituality in Christians and which ones contribute to unhealthy spirituality? Why? What criteria did you use to decide on healthy and unhealthy spirituality?

2. *Sexual Identity Group:* Which ideas help to build healthy, Christian sexual identity and which ones contribute to an unhealthy sexual identity? How? For lesbians? For gay men? For heterosexuals? For youth who are not yet certain of their sexual identity? Why? What criteria did you use to decide on healthy and unhealthy sexual identity?

Step Two:

Compare the responses with the larger group. Try to develop ten strategies for building and maintaining Christian traditions that nurture healthy spirituality as well as healthy sexual identity.

TAKING NOTE

Journal the answers to the following questions:

- Throughout your life are there any ways in which you have changed your mind about what is best for you in your own sexual practices and desires?

- If change has occurred, has your Christian faith been part of that process of changing your mind? Why or why not?

- If you have not changed your mind, is Christian faith a resource for you as you reflect on the ways your physical sexual responses and desires have evolved throughout your life? Why or why not?

Closing Prayer and Song

Give thanks to God by naming all of the Christian saints (living and deceased) who have helped create valuable Christian tradition, especially concerning Christian faith and sexuality. Include the names of loved ones, mentors, and pioneers in the church and society in your prayer.

Conclude the prayer time by singing "For All the Saints."

Assignments for Next Session

1. Identify the use of experience, scripture, tradition, and reason in the skit that we did during this session. Think about how they are connected to each other within the skit. How does one depend upon the other?

2. Review your "taking note" journaling for all of the previous sessions.

3. Read the introduction to the next session (page 113).

4. Watch *Priest* by Miramax films, which portrays gripping issues of ministry and sexuality.

5. Read Erin's story.

❧ ERIN'S STORY

It's clear that when the topic of gender identity is on the table we all have something at stake, for we all must deal with what it means to be gendered as male or female. So when I speak of myself as transgender, or Gwen Araujo, one of Newark's youth recently murdered because she was transgender, I am talking about a subject that in one way or another affects us all.

Most of us are lucky. In the words of Presbyterian minister Mister Fred Rogers, we are born male, feel like boys and men, and are attracted to females. Or, we are born female, feel like girls and women, and are attracted to boys. For the small, but very real, number of us for whom this does not happen, the world becomes a dangerous place filled with ridicule, rejection, and violence. Gwen felt that violence a few months ago at the hands of supposed friends — a violence bred, I believe, in the determined ignorance of our churches and communities who refuse to face the reality of gender and its diverse expressions, preferring to enforce artificial gender expectations on children already overstressed with the task of growing up. Gwen was an attractive, outgoing, seventeen-year-old transgender young woman, excited about life and her future. What a contrast when I think of myself at that age, a boy painfully shy and withdrawn, dangerously depressed, and wracked with guilt over my own gender confusion. I felt violent toward myself; Gwen experienced the violence of others. And in a way the perpetrators of Gwen's murder, children all, are as much victims as Gwen and I, their lives destroyed by the fear and ignorance we all share.

How does one speak rationally in this world about such a pervasive and yet little understood topic as gender identity? Embedded deep within the fabric of our society are assumptions about what it means to be male or female that lie at the bedrock of our cultural institutions, most especially the church. The first words we hear in life are a fateful pronouncement of this reality. "It's a boy!" or "it's a girl!" comes the blessing. A blessing, that is, if your sense of being a boy or a girl, a man or a woman, fits the label given. And woe unto you if even this pronouncement, this first category, cannot be established because some twist of biology has caused your anatomical sex to be indeterminate. We are only now beginning to resist our corporate temptation to surgically — violently — impress an acceptable gender onto the bodies of these *intersex* infants, a way of assuaging our anxiety over our compulsive needs for them to be clearly gendered as either male or female.

It's a daunting task as Christians, to change the world's perception — "neither male nor female," from God's perspective. Like the religious people of biblical times, we resist overcoming boundaries: clean and unclean, welcomed and outcast, male and female. But then that's exactly what a poor carpenter's son from Nazareth asked of us.

—Erin K. Swenson, white marriage therapist
and Presbyterian pastor[59]

Session Six

Building Good Community, Keeping Faith

"En resumén, todo se reduce a credibilidad." (It all comes down to trust.) Without trust we can't adequately respond to God's call to be loving and justice-oriented people. Trust is essential for us to build a good community within our churches, and in the world we share with people of many religious faiths and traditions.

In the previous sessions we have worked together to reflect on theological resources for our Christian faith. While working together, there have probably been moments when some of us have felt a renewed sense of hope. Taking this time to probe our understandings of Christian faith and sexuality has led to wonderful discoveries, among them that new ways to have conversations help to build stronger bonds of community within the church.

However, some of us also wonder if we are capable of genuinely trusting one another in lasting ways, over the long haul of our lives together. There is still a significant degree of fearfulness, hostility, woundedness, alienation, and impatience within the broader church, and perhaps within this study group as well. Will we trust one another enough to build a community that affirms lesbians, gay men, bisexuals, and transgender persons who are in our families, pulpits, pews, high schools, and workplaces? Will we have enough trust to directly challenge each other on the heterosexist/gender identity assumptions and homophobic attitudes that are part of our parenting practices, our Confirmation class curriculum, and our own sense of self-worth?

"¿Cómo podemos lidiar con los conflictos que se producen en este proceso de construir una comunidad?" (How do we handle the conflict that comes with this kind of community-building work?) Can we differ with one another without inflicting more wounds, alienation from church life, and emotional exhaustion? Some of us are already sick of the racism of white gay rights activists; sick of the rejection within our own racial/ethnic communities; sick of the self-righteousness of those on "the other side"; sick of liberal sexual ethics and theology that devalues the Bible; sick of the sexism of men, no matter what their sexual orientation might be; sick of having to explain what it means to consider oneself bisexual, transgender, or queer; sick of spending time on insular denominational politics about sexuality rather than on Christian witness and evangelism in our world; sick of listening to other Christians try to make us feel ashamed of ourselves, or of our daughters and sons. What does it mean to differ with one another in these ways, and, at the same time, continue to try to build trust between us?

It's only possible to build trust if we do not ignore the emotional and spiritual needs each of us brings. We crave affirmation and acceptance in a community that shares our commitment to Christian faith, and we must remember that there is a wellspring of hope in that shared commitment. Our Christian faith grants us permission to differ with each other and even fosters the ways in which we *are* different from each other. There is excitement and inspiration for us in learning from those differences by listening to each other. Making these discoveries about one another can teach us about God's amazing grace and creativity. Also, we can be blessed with tremendous support and encouragement when learning collectively as a group that is struggling with issues of faith and sexuality side by side.

Of course, sexuality is an intensely personal matter so we do not want to share everything that we are learning with the entire group. But the whole community benefits from individuals learning about ourselves in relation to God and neighbor, which takes place when we focus on sexuality issues. We are grateful for the effort that each one of us expends separately as well as the risks that we have taken by entering into dialogue.

During the past few sessions we've found ways to talk about topics like divorce, safe-sex discussions with youth, sodomy, and masturbation in relation to our Christian faith. We have been able to discuss our use of experience, scripture, tradition, and reason in cultivating our Christian faith. But we still need to practice our ability to put these resources in conversation with each other. As we develop Christian understandings of sexual orientation, how do these four resources work together? In the midst of conflicts and intolerance, how do these resources help us to build trust, find hope, and respond to God's call to reach out to all of our neighbors with a gentle, loving spirit?

GATHERING

Opening Scripture and Prayer (Facilitator's Guide, page 147)

Read 1 Corinthians 12:12–17, 24b–27

Body Prayer: Let us join in a prayer that allows us to use our body, mind, and spirit. (Facilitator's Guide, page 147)

Step One:

Remove your shoes and gather to join together (literally) for the Lord's Prayer.

Follow the instructions below for attaching yourselves to one another. Make appropriate adjustments to the directions for differently abled members of your group.

- The first person joins one hand to a second person's elbow.
- That second person joins her or his head to a third person's foot.
- That third person extends one finger and lightly touches a fourth person's shoulder.

- That fourth person holds hands with a fifth person, while the fourth person's other hand is outstretched and waving to the outside world to come in the door.

- The fifth person stands with his or her back touching a sixth person.

The remaining people should attach themselves to any two people in the group, with one foot touching one person and one hand touching another person. Make sure that no one is left without having at least one person touching him or her.

Step Two:

Say the Lord's Prayer together.

INFORMING

Let's review the meaning of the four resources for Christian faith we have been studying, and think about how they are interrelated.

Exercise 1: "All Four of Them Come to Visit!"
(Facilitator's Guide, page 148)

To review the four resources — reason, experience, scripture, tradition — talk to each other as if you have become the embodiment of these resources.

Step One:

Divide participants into four groups and assign each group one of the following: experience, scripture, tradition, and reason. Spread out into four corners of the room, one group in each corner. Each group should take a few minutes to remind themselves in what ways they are an important resource for Christian faith. To get started, complete the sentence,

Scripture [or Tradition, or Reason, or Experience] supplies Christian faith with . . .

Beulah met Daniel at a predominantly Mexican church in El Paso, Texas. They were married and had children: a daughter, Gloria (in 1947), and two sons. When they moved out of the city to a suburb, Beulah recalls that as an interracial couple, "I didn't see the prejudice as much as he did....It took me a long time to realize how much prejudice there was. I was pretty naïve." Years later, a letter from their daughter informed her parents that she was a lesbian. Gloria was living with her lover. "Because we were coming to see her, she wanted to tell us....I was a bit uncomfortable at first. But I liked the woman she was with; we both really liked her a lot." Beulah has not found her church a welcoming place for her and her family. "One Sunday when my grandchildren were with me in church, the pastor started talking against homosexuality. The grandchildren all know their aunt is gay, and they talked with me about the sermon. They were upset because they love their aunt, and here was a pastor talking against her." Remembering the incident, Beulah sighs. "I'm still waiting for the church to catch up with everyone else when it comes to homosexuality."

—*Beulah, white, eighty-three-year-old grandmother*[60]

Step Two:

One at a time, each group goes to the center of the room. As one group stands in the center, the other three groups take turns telling them why they are needed to express Christian faith. Each group only needs to come up with one statement about why they need the group in the middle.

For example, if the scripture group were in the center, the tradition group might tell the scripture group, "Scripture, we need
you because you inspire our actions," or "Scripture, we need you
in order to . . ." Then the experience group would add examples of
how scripture is needed to inform experience. In a slight variation
on this pattern, the reason group might tell the scripture group
why and how it makes them feel like a useful tool in interpretation
of scripture, saying: "Scripture, you make us feel useful because
you allow us to . . ."

The process is repeated until all four groups have had a turn
in the center of the room.

Step Three:

Draw the connections. Based upon what you've heard in this exercise, draw a diagram that illustrates how these four resources
of faith are dependent upon each other. The only words allowed
on your diagram are: experience, scripture, tradition, reason. Be
creative!

Exercise 2: Learning from David's Story
(Facilitator's Guide, page 148)

Now we have some definitions and diagrams, but what does this
discussion have to do with our sexuality and everyday lives? To
better recognize how experience, scripture, tradition, and reason
are interdependent resources within one's individual life, let's read
a story from *One More River to Cross: Black and Gay in America.*[61]

Step One:

Choose three people to read the following story aloud, taking the
roles of Narrator, David, and Minister.

Narrator: David, a black gay man in Washington, describes the
days before and after his friend died of AIDS in the summer of
1995. David remembers Vaughn's mother as being "sweet" when
he met her in the hospital, but says that her attitude changed
when Vaughn passed away. She resisted David's efforts to find a

minister to perform the funeral service and instead insisted on her own minister. She also rejected Vaughn's wish that David sing at the funeral. In the middle of the service, the minister called for congregants to come to the altar if they wanted to dedicate their lives to Jesus. Finding that no one answered the call after several repeated requests, the minister told the organist to stop playing and decided to speak candidly to the congregation.

Minister: "We all know what Vaughn died of..."

Narrator: the minister said. Eyeballing a contingent of a dozen black men sitting together, the minister warned that more people would die if they did not dedicate their lives to Jesus....

Minister: "Who in this church is saved? Raise your hands if you've been saved."

Narrator: David raised his hand, and the minister glared at him with disbelief.

Minister: "How could you be saved?"

David: "I've accepted the Lord in my life and glorify and praise him."

Narrator: David responded.

Minister: "Son, the Bible says that homosexuality is an abomination in the eyes of the Lord. Vaughn is on his way to hell, and you will be too if don't change your ways..."

Narrator: the minister told him.

David: "The Bible says, 'Judge not that ye be judged...'"

Narrator: David retorted keeping his composure, but all the while shocked that this exchange was occurring in church, at a funeral, with Vaughn's mother sitting there quietly.... David recalled that when the casket was removed, "People walked outside like nothing happened." No one even apologized. As David learned that day, religion carries enormous influence over the lives of black people.

Step Two:

Work in small groups to answer the following questions about the story.

1. There are several elements of tension and conflict in this story, between David and Vaughn's mother, Vaughn's mother and Vaughn (perhaps?), David and the minister, David and the rest of the congregation. How do the tension and conflict in this story make you feel? Why?

2. David and the minister use the resources of experience, scripture, tradition, and reason to explain their faith. Identify how and when these resources were invoked. How do they overlap and work together when used by each character? What are the differences and similarities in how each character uses them?

3. What would you do? If you were placed in the same situation as David, how would experience, scripture, tradition, and reason be resources for you? What would you do that was similar to or different from David's actions? Why?

Step Three:

Share insights from the small groups with the larger group. On newsprint, make a list of the overlapping ways that experience, scripture, tradition, and reason work together either in the story or for group members as they imagine themselves in the same situation.

Going Deeper Exercise: "You're the Pastor"

Step One:

Count off by threes and assign each person in your group to be "the pastor" for one of the following scenarios. All of the ones will be the pastor for scenario one, all of the twos will be the pastor for scenario two, and all of the threes are the pastor for scenario three.

Step Two:

Each person should read their assigned scenario where they will pretend to be the pastor being sought out. Prepare to tell the whole group what you would say in this situation; you *must* use scripture, reason, tradition, and experience in your response.

Step Three:

Read the scenarios aloud, one at a time. Take turns giving responses, but the pastor should speak as if she or he is talking directly to the person who came for advice. If it would make this easier, have someone in the group sit in front of the person who is pretending to be the pastor.

Note: This is not a role-play, simply a chance to practice a few sentences that would use the four resources of faith in pastoral situations.

> *Scenario 1:* You are a local church pastor. A fifty-year-old, white, heterosexual woman in your congregation comes to talk with you about whether or not to invite Christian families that include same-sex partners and their children to participate in Sunday school. These families live in the neighborhood of the church. She definitely wants to invite these families, but fears that they will not be treated well by the Sunday school teachers who vocally oppose "the sin of homosexuality."

> *Scenario 2:* You are a campus minister, and a twenty-year-old Latina college student whose sexual orientation you do not know comes to talk to you about why the church is "so hypocritical." She complains about how the church talks about all of this "love your neighbor as yourself stuff" and says "we are all one body in Christ," and then it won't even consider allowing people who feel called to the ministry to become ordained, unless they are heterosexual.

> *Scenario 3:* You are a local church pastor, and a white gay man who is a member of your church comes to talk to you

about how to cope with the sexual problems caused by his life partner's illness. His life partner has recovered from prostate cancer but is no longer able to function sexually in the same way that he did before his surgery. This parishioner asks you to help him arrive at a Christian understanding of what is a fair and loving response to the situation that also honors the sexual desire they both have.

FOCUSING

How do we address conflicts related to faith and sexuality, not only as individuals, but as an entire faith community? Let's practice our theological skills in a situation where there is conflict among members in a local church that is related to both sexual orientation and racial/ethnic identity. Let's also practice Christian Conferencing as a way of addressing that conflict. Christian Conferencing is a process of discernment for group decision making that involves prayer and dialogue with one another until consensus can be reached among members of the group.

Exercise 3: A Christian Conferencing Fishbowl
(Facilitator's Guide, page 149)

Step One:

Select six people to be the "actors" in the role-play and sit in the center of the room to role-play a staff-parish committee making a decision about hiring a new assistant minister. The remaining members of the group will be the observers. Read the description of the situation and assign the six perspectives below to the "actors." The facilitator allows the role-play to continue for about twenty minutes. Participants should be conscious of allowing everyone to have a chance to speak and let the facilitator worry about keeping time. When the facilitator stops the discussion, applaud the actors!

The committee makes their decision through a process of Christian Conferencing. For them, Christian Conferencing includes time for prayer, time for silence, time for respectfully listening to a range of views without debating each other (i.e., without offering direct responses to each other), and decision making by arriving at consensus (no voting). The chairperson offers prayer when needed, calls for silence when appropriate, and facilitates the decision making based on the views that are presented.

Each committee member draws from experience, scripture, tradition, and reason to present their viewpoints about what to do in this situation.

Role-play: A multiracial, middle-class to working-class, four-hundred-member congregation with one pastor has made a special commitment. They have decided to hire a part-time assistant minister for one year to help them truly listen to the Holy Spirit for their understanding of issues related to homosexuality. These issues touch the lives of their church members in varied ways. This additional church staff member will lead and organize communal prayer meetings, small group Bible studies, "holy conversations" that bring people together with differing views, and help with outreach to bring in perspectives that are not already represented in the congregation. The church wants to do Christian community-building work that nurtures their faith in God within their own church and possibly beyond it with other local congregations. The church has made a commitment to reduce every item of their annual church budget by a certain percentage in order to make the funds available to pay this part-time minister for one year. The staff-parish committee has to decide between two finalists for the position, both highly qualified with experience in and sensitivity to the concerns of the congregation and seminary-trained. The finalists are a partnered, white lesbian and an unmarried, Asian, heterosexual man.

The following views are represented on the committee:

1. Hire the man: Hiring a white woman for the position represents an abandonment of the church's commitment to make antiracism part of every ministry in the church. Hiring an Asian man ensures racial/ethnic sensitivity, which is crucial in this multiracial church.

2. Hire the woman: Hiring an "out" lesbian ensures genuine sensitivity to issues of homosexuality, which is an absolute necessity for someone in this position.

3. Don't hire either one: The church should be hiring someone to work on issues of hunger and poverty, which are much more pressing in the world as well as most significant to Jesus in the Christian gospel.

4. Don't hire either one: Neither hiring a lesbian nor a single heterosexual minister offers a healthy, positive image that a married heterosexual minister would bring to this job.

5. (Chairperson) Hire either one: It doesn't matter which one is selected; just make sure that the committee does not destroy the hard work that was done to get the congregation to take the bold and proactive step of making this commitment.

6. Pastor: Agrees with the chairperson but in this role-play is not allowed to communicate verbally, but can gesture and use facial expressions.

Step Two:

When the facilitator stops the role-play, come together and share your experience.

1. What did you feel?

   For participants: How did it feel to be in the middle of the room with others watching you? What range of emotions did you experience in this process — frustrated, angered, uncertain, uncomfortable? What made you feel uneasy or self-conscious?

   For observers: How did it feel to be watching others without being able to enter into the conversation? What made you feel uneasy or especially glad that you didn't have to be in the spotlight with those in the middle?

2. How was the process of Christian Conferencing?

   For the entire group: What are the strengths and weaknesses of Christian Conferencing for developing trust? What aspects of Christian Conferencing diminished trust in the committee? What increased trust? What additional ideas do you have about what could have increased trust in this situation?

Step Three:

Form smaller groups of three or four to discuss the power dynamics in this process related to sexual orientation, race/ethnicity, and God's presence.

1. When trying to make decisions about who should be included in the church, issues of race/ethnicity and sexual orientation are sometimes pitted against each other as if they represent opposing concerns. This usually fosters destructive debates, competition about oppression, and most importantly a doomed attempt to try to divide aspects of our identity and experience (our racial/ethnic backgrounds and our sexuality) into unrelated, separate parts. Instead, let's learn from the power dynamics that surround issues of race/ethnicity and sexual orientation in our church and society. Power dynamics are often expressed in how some people are marginalized by being labeled as "the problem" to be helped or solved, while other people are normalized, viewed as having no problems requiring community attention, and given respect and credibility automatically (without having to earn it).

   a. In relation to race/ethnicity in this church meeting *and* in the broader society, who is seen as "the problem" and who are seen as "the normal" ones? Who has more credibility, status, or influence, and who has less? Why?

   b. In relation to sexual orientation in this church meeting and in the broader society, who is seen as "the problem" and who are seen as "the normal" ones? Who has more credibility, status, or influence, and who has less? Why?

c. What's helpful about making comparisons between race/ ethnicity and sexual orientation, and what can be hurtful?

2. Where is God within these power dynamics related to race/ ethnicity and sexuality? Name the ways God's power was present for the committee. Describe how God was calling the committee to be accountable to God and how God's power was available to the members of the committee. Gather the whole group and conclude by singing "Spirit of the Living God."

TAKING NOTE

It's time to take note of the fact that it's the last session, that we made it to the end! Hurray!

1. Evaluate your experience of this entire study. What did you appreciate most about this study? What was most challenging about it? What did you appreciate least about this study?

    What is the most important thing that you learned about your Christian faith from doing this study?

2. Sign a covenant statement about how you will share what you learned:

    I, _____, will carry the voices of LGBT persons and their families that I met in this book to _____, where I work and socialize. I will continue to pursue my questions about how I use experience, scripture, tradition, and reason when articulating my faith, especially related to sexuality issues, with _____, and in _____.

    So that I can continue the conversations that we began in this group, I will experiment with mentioning faith and sexuality in some new ways to _____.

    Signature: _____

Going Deeper: Dance Prayer

Celebrate the end of your work as a group with dancing. Celebrate God's gift of sexuality with a dance-prayer. One of the best exercises that reflects a truly embodied theology is "The Hokey Pokey." Play some Christian rap music (for example, Kirk Franklin) or Christian rock music and dance as a group:

> Put your *right foot* in, put your *right foot* out.
>
> Put your *right foot* in, and shake it all about.
>
> You do the Hokey Pokey, and
>
> You turn yourself about.
>
> (And that's what it's all about!)
>
> (Next: Left foot, then right hand, then left hand, then head, then whole self)

Then, discuss: Was that prayer? Why or why not?

Because we've been in deep conversation with each other, we have been forever changed by it. We acknowledge God's holy presence in what has occurred even though, right now, we don't know all of the ways that our lives have been touched and altered by these conversations. We give thanks for each other, and for God illumined in and through each other.

Ritual of Gratitude for the Group

Step One:

Place candles in a bowl filled with sand. Gather the group in a circle.

Step Two:

One at a time, each person lights a candle and then says: "I have let my light shine and I will continue to let it shine in our world." The group responds: "You have let your light shine and it has illumined our lives."

Step Three:

After the group has responded, turn to the next person and hold the bowl while she or he lights a candle, repeats the refrain, and the group responds. Repeat until everyone has had a turn.

Closing Prayer

Thank you God for being with us at all times and in all places. As we try to build a good community, we place our trust in you, the abundant, unceasing wellspring for all our hopes and faith. As we talk about the meaning of sexuality we place our trust in you, the amazing author of human sexuality.

We give you thanks for the resources of our experience, scripture, tradition, and powers of reason. We give you thanks for the ways that they inform our Christian faith and help us to articulate it in our daily witness of discipleship.

Help us to go forward with what we have learned and experienced in this group to have more appreciation for the gift of sexuality you have given to us. Help us to build a more just and compassionate world for lesbians, bisexuals, transgender persons, heterosexuals, and gay men, across all racial/ethnic and national backgrounds.

We pray in the name of Jesus Christ, our Savior and our Friend. Amen.

Facilitator's Guide

FACILITATOR'S GUIDE TO SESSION ONE: Can We Talk?

Materials Needed

- Newsprint, markers
- Hymn/song books
- Easels with newsprint for Pictionary
- One-minute timer
- Bibles (at least one New Revised Standard Version)
- Blank pages for journaling

Preparation

- Write one "hopes and fears" question on each piece of newsprint (see p. 37). Arrange the sheets of newsprint and markers throughout the room and arrange the room so that participants can move freely to each station.
- Set up Pictionary easel with newsprint and markers.

Opening Prayer (page 27)

Begin by thanking all the participants for their attendance and share the opening prayer. Read the prayer aloud as a group or select one person (rotate each session) to read the prayer for the group.

Exercise 1: Introductions (page 28)

The purpose of this style of introductions is to begin building trust among participants and to have fun. It will help if participants choose to share with their partners unusual pieces of information about themselves, thus making the false information more difficult to determine. This exercise also helps underscore the ease and difficulty of lying about ourselves.

Exercise 2: A Covenant for Discussion (page 29)

It is very important that the group establish its own rules of conduct, enter into a covenant with one another, and symbolize this agreement through ritual. Therefore, resist the temptation to assume such guidelines are common sense and need not be made explicit. Skipping this exercise bypasses an opportunity to build trust, avoids the very real issues of vulnerability when sharing who we are, and eliminates a powerful tool for the facilitator to use in future sessions when conflict arises.

Assume conflict will arise, and affirm the group's ability to stick with one another through the uneasiness. Affirm that it's acceptable for issues not to be fully resolved and for participants to disagree with one another. However, do not allow comments that attack, demean, or assault another person's character, as these destroy rather than build trust.

Review the covenant with any new member(s) that join after the first meeting and have them add their name(s) to indicate their agreement.

When the rules are broken, step in immediately yet gently and offer guidance to return to the task at hand by a comment such as: "We'll want to remember the covenant that we agreed to as we . . . " If someone is monopolizing the conversation try: "Thank you for your input; now let's hear from some other people." If a person persists, use that person's name: "Thank you, Ed. We want to make sure we hear from everyone else." Then be careful to make eye contact with others but not with the person monopolizing the conversation. You may also want to move into small groups and specifically prompt the group by asking: "Has everyone had a chance to speak?" In a small group, you may even assign (to the most talkative member of the group) the task of making sure everyone has had input.

Remember that there are some people who may need to sit back and be quiet before engaging in the conversation. Offer such persons an opportunity for input by asking them specifically by name if they wish to add something or if they wish to pass.

Expect Discomfort (page 30)

As an introduction to the next activity, participants should read "The Difficulty of the Discussion" section on page 13 if they have not already done so. Acknowledging the discomfort in the room around discussing any sexuality, much less sexual orientation issues, may help alleviate such discomfort or at the very least affirm that such discomfort is normal. Be sensitive to signs of discomfort throughout the group and be ready to discuss these feelings with participants. Reassure them that discomfort is common.

Exercise 3: Pictionary (page 30)

Write the following words on a piece of paper (one word per piece) and provide one word at a time to the volunteer selected to illustrate the word on the newsprint for their team. Give each team sixty seconds to guess the word the presenter is drawing. You may wish to keep score, but it is not primarily a competitive event. It is meant to introduce terminology that might otherwise be uncomfortable to bring up or difficult to define. Standard rules apply: do not use numbers, letters, or verbal clues.

SCRIPTURE	JESUS	CLIMAX
LESBIAN	HETEROSEXUAL	RELIGION
INCARNATION	CONVERSATION	TRADITION
CONFLICT	EMBRACE	INTIMACY
	THEOLOGY	

Exercise 4: Resources of Faith (page 31)

Divide class into four groups. Assign each group one the four resources of faith: scripture, tradition, experience, or reason. Follow the steps of the exercise listed on page 32.

Exercise 5: How Do We Discuss Sexuality? What Is It? (page 33)

Invite participants to read the quotations about sexuality (silently or aloud depending on the size of the group) and encourage each person to write down words or phrases that stand out for them. Direct each person to write down the general idea of sexuality they received from the quotations. This allows all participants to record their under-standings without interference from the most talkative or outgoing members of the group. It also encourages participants to record their "starting point" impressions. These will be useful later in the study to compare how their impressions have changed.

Exercise 6: Risky Scriptures (page 35)

For each of the four scripture passages listed, choose a volunteer to read the text aloud. Encourage participants to listen to the text without comment; some of these texts will be examined in more detail in a later session. Those who have personally struggled with these texts, or those who have had these texts used against them, may find it extremely difficult to hear them again. Acknowledge that it may be painful for some to hear these texts. Include a moment of silence following each reading to allow the participants to write down their responses to the questions.

It is important to point out that interpreting scripture is risk-taking work. Studying scripture may even be a painful experience. It requires prayerful discernment as well as scholarly examination.

This exercise also helps participants understand their own social location (i.e., how who they are impacts how they perceive things and interpret scripture). Such work lays a crucial foundation for the later focus on scripture and its meaning for our lives.

Exercise 7: Our Hopes and Fears (page 37)

Post five pieces of newsprint around the room with markers at each station. On each piece of paper, write one of the following questions for participants to answer:

- What fears do I have about participating in this discussion?
- What is one hope that I have for this study?
- How might this conversation nurture my faith?
- If someone in my family "came out" to me as homosexual, my response would be...

Encourage participants to take no more than ten minutes to circulate around the room and write their responses to each question on the newsprint. Participants need not follow any particular order in answering the questions. Part of the process is the random chaos created when participants are allowed to consider the question, read others' responses and provide their own answers. When time is up, explain that their responses will be read in the next session as part of the opening prayer.

Journaling

Explain that each session will follow the format of GIFT: Gathering, Informing, Focusing, and Taking note (see page 21).

Give participants a few minutes to further consider and journal their response to the question, "How might this conversation and study nurture my faith?" Participants may want to use blank paper or a journal for their responses.

Assignments for Next Session (page 37)

To prepare for the next session, invite participants to complete the assigned homework. While it may seem impossible and silly to use "sexuality" and "theology" in the same sentence, it will help folks understand how unnatural discussing sexuality in a theological context has become. It may also help them overcome their discomfort or affirm the importance of their participation in such a discussion.

Closing Song and Prayer (page 38)

As the members of the group become more comfortable with one another, you may want to include a time for people to lift up intercessions spontaneously either before the prayer or as part of the prayer time.

FACILITATOR'S GUIDE
TO SESSION TWO:
Are We Theologians?

Materials Needed

- "Fears and Hopes" newsprint answers from the last session (post)
- Bibles (including NRSV)
- Masking Tape
- Hymn/song books
- Paper and Pencils

Opening Prayer, Scripture, and Song (page 49)

Welcome people as they gather. Remind them of the importance of honoring the covenant to start and end on time. Using the responses from the last session on participants' fears and hopes for this study, create together a short opening prayer.

Have someone read aloud 1 John 1:1. Then sing a song about one's personal relationship with God that is familiar to your community.

If there are new members present, ask if they are willing to enter into the covenant; if they are, ask them to sign the list.

Today's Theme — Popcorn Style (page 49)

Check to see if participants have had the opportunity to read the introduction. Offer them a few moments to review. Then start with a time of "popcorning." "Popcorn" is a way to allow participants to say, without censure or comment from the rest of the group, ideas or phrases that caught their attention. Try to encourage short and quick responses from the group.

Exercise 1: I Have Permission! (page 50)

This session challenges people to speak aloud about issues and topics most churches work hard to avoid. Many folks might be embarrassed by the topics or confused about their own beliefs about sexuality.

I Have Permission! is a way to help folks articulate those things that may be difficult or awkward.

Exercise 2: Ages and Stages of Faith Development (page 50)

Most people are unaware that their beliefs have changed over the course of their lifetimes. This exercise helps individuals see that. Ask people to choose two distinct ages in their life and place each age in one of the boxes. Write in each box answers to the questions related to their beliefs at that time. In small groups, have people share their faith development. In the larger group, answer the discussion questions.

Exercise 3: I Believe . . . (page 54)

Give the group five minutes to write their individual statements of faith. When they are finished, ask them to share their statements in small groups while answering the discussion questions.

Exercise 4: Playing at a Church Council Near You (page 55)

Assign roles to group members for the role-play. Give the group a five-minute break so each actor can consider his or her part. At the conclusion of the break, begin the role-play. Role-play the church meeting for no more than ten minutes. At the conclusion, ask the observers only (if the group is large enough, otherwise include the entire group) to discuss the first four questions. Then have the entire group answer the remaining questions together.

Journaling and Closing (pages 57–58)

- Give the group approximately five minutes to journal.

- Sing a hymn or song of the group's choosing.

- Ask if there are any questions about the homework for the coming session.

- For the closing prayer, offer one-sentence "Thank you" prayers.

FACILITATOR'S GUIDE TO SESSION THREE: Experience

Materials Needed

- Bibles
- Hymn/song books
- Newsprint, tape
- Paper, markers, pencils
- Candle, matches

Preparation

Post newsprint, divided into two columns. Label columns "Authentic" and "Inauthentic."

Exercise 1: Do You See What I See? (page 64)

This first exercise is designed to help participants understand that our experience of the same thing often differs. Allow them a few minutes of silence to interpret what they are viewing, then lead discussion.

Exercise 2: Authentic Experience (page 66)

Begin by having participants read aloud the two passages describing religious experience. Then answer the questions in small groups.

Exercise 3: My Authentic Experience (page 67)

Ask the group to ponder in silence the questions listed. Invite members to write poems about their experience of God and share them with the group.

Exercise 4: Inside Out! (page 68)

This exercise helps group members gain insight into the experiences of gay men and lesbians in a heterosexually dominated culture.

Ask the participants to get as comfortable as possible, close their eyes, breathe deeply, relaxing more and more completely with each breath, and as they sink into the rhythm of their breathing, let go of whatever thoughts may be distracting them from full relaxation. Read this slowly to allow participants to fully experience this meditation.

If you are heterosexual, imagine what it means to be heterosexual in a society where homosexuality is the natural order of things. If you are a lesbian, gay man, or bisexual person, imagine how your world would change now that you are in a majority and your sexuality is the norm.

Imagine waking up one morning and that everyone in your house is a lesbian or gay man. As you prepare for work, you turn on the TV. The morning news show has stories related to gay men and lesbians. All the ads and commercials use lesbian and gay actors to sell products.

Leaving for work, you listen to a radio station. The morning DJ's jokes are snide references to heterosexuality. Clearly, he disapproves. As the music plays, a man's voice raps about "how much I love him." Note how this makes you feel.

Thinking back, you realize that throughout your whole life, being gay or lesbian was celebrated, while heterosexuality was treated like a dirty secret no one talked about. Your teachers in school were lesbians and gay men. The majority of the people you learned about — inventors, scientists, politicians — were lesbians and gay men. Occasionally, someone would talk about the "rare exception of a heterosexual" who made a positive contribution to our society. The kids at school regularly taunted each other with slurs about being "a breeder" or "hetero."

Even in church the message was clear: being heterosexual is a sin. Religious leaders were emphatic about the sin of Adam and Eve and that therefore it is sinful for a man to lie with a woman. Clearly, God's will for humankind is to be lesbian and gay. Being heterosexual is considered unnatural, incompatible with the teachings of the church. Heterosexuals must have had traumas in their lives that make them act the way they do. Some people think it is a mental illness that can be cured. If you are heterosexual, note how this makes you feel. If you are gay or lesbian, note how this makes you feel.

Government is totally run by lesbians and gay men. There is not one heterosexual congressperson. Once, a heterosexual ran for vice president, and that really shook things up! Political commentators asked how this would affect America's credibility to other countries. Leaders were wondering aloud what kind of message this would send to our children, and what kind of values this would spread. In response, elected officials signed legislation forbidding any affirmation of the "heterosexual lifestyle" in the public schools. The president, a gay man, signed the Defense of Values Act, restricting heterosexuals from the right to marry or receive legal privileges that marriage brings.

Feel what it is like that lesbians and gay men are the leaders, the power centers, the prime movers. As you grow up, you are taught that heterosexuals are evil and unnatural, that all they are interested in is sex, and that they will molest children. Being a gay man or a lesbian is considered morally superior to being heterosexual. Settling down with a same-sex partner is considered the most authentic expression of our nature.

Of course, as you grow up, it's natural to have some confusion over your sexual identity and to question these strict messages you've been taught. You struggle with the roles that are defined for you as a lesbian or gay man by society. Psychologists are emphatic that heterosexuality can be cured. Therapy is recommended to help those with heterosexual tendencies make adjustments so they can reject those tendencies and embrace their true nature. The therapy is administered by a lesbian, who has the education and wisdom to know what's best for you. Some heteros learn to "pass," dating someone of the same sex to "prove" that they are like everyone else. Note how this makes you feel.

Everywhere you look — newspapers, books, television, advertisements, movies — the message is clear: being a lesbian or gay man is the norm while heterosexuals are condemned. But you are who you are. What choices do you make? How do you live your life? What do you like about this new world? What do you dislike? Sit and experience this new world for a few more minutes. Reflect on your feelings. When you are ready, open your eyes and return to the group.

This may be an emotional exercise for some people. Remind people that they do not have to share if they are not comfortable doing so. Lead a discussion based on the questions listed on page 68.[62]

Taking Note (page 69)

Allow time for participants to journal their answers to the listed questions.

Assignments for Next Session (page 69)

Review assignments for the next session with the group. Ask if there are any questions about the assignments.

FACILITATOR'S GUIDE TO SESSION FOUR: Scripture

Materials Needed

- Hymn or song books
- Individual pieces of paper marked with the following words, with one word per paper:

  LET ALL THAT YOU DO BE DONE IN LOVE 1 COR. 16:14.

  This may be changed according to group size, and there should be one piece of paper for each participant.

- Blank sheets of paper
- Crayons or markers
- Tape
- Candle, matches

Opening (page 80)

Exercise 1: What Does It Say? (page 80)

The purpose of this activity is to have participants correctly create the following verse from the words they have been given:

> Let all that you do be done in love. (1 Cor. 16:14)

Give each participant a piece of paper with one word from the scripture verse written on it. Without speaking, participants are to figure out how the words go together to create a verse from scripture. Please note the number of participants you have. Some of the words can be combined for smaller groups. We suggest, for instance, combining "1 Cor. 16:14," or leaving the scripture reference out altogether if the group is smaller.

When the group has completed the task, let them know if they put the scripture together correctly or not. Then lead them in the discussion questions.

Exercise 2: The Family Bible (page 81)

Hand out paper and crayons or markers. Ask people to close their eyes and remember the religious traditions of their family. In particular, what discussions did the family have that were biblically based? Was there a family Bible? Where was it kept? What was it used for? Some may not have any recollections; that's okay. It will still inform the next step of the exercise: invite the group members to draw a picture that represents how their family used the Bible. Some may depict the Bible filled with drying flowers! Others may completely omit it from their drawing. There is no right or wrong depiction. Have group members share their pictures, and then answer the discussion questions.

Exercise 3: Reading the Bible with Our Hearts and Our Minds (page 81)

Have a member of the group read aloud the introduction to this segment. Invite the group to respond to the discussion questions.

Exercise 4: Yada, Yada, Yada (page 83)

This exercise can help participants see how other parts of the Bible can open up the meaning of a particular passage. Genesis 19 is one of the seven passages that have traditionally been interpreted as condemning homosexuality. Divide the group into two smaller groups. One group will answer the study questions based on the text itself. The other group will answer the questions based not only on the Genesis 19 passage, but also on what other passages say about Sodom.

This should create a lively discussion!

Exercise 5: Body Charades (page 86)

Here are some words to spell out:

KISS   ROMANCE   SEX   BODY   BUTTOCKS   LOVE

Journaling

Give group members a few minutes to complete the Taking Note questions.

Closing Prayer (page 87)

It may be uncomfortable for some participants to say aloud what they are thankful for about sex. Give permission for folks to offer silent prayers as the candle is passed to them.

FACILITATOR'S GUIDE TO SESSION FIVE: Sex and Tradition

Materials Needed

- Posterboard and magic markers or presentation software to project the group's ideas
- Clay
- Construction paper, scissors

- Pencil and paper
- A large platter for each member of the group
- Note cards of six different colors
- Newsprint, markers, tape
- Chairs that are easy to move around

Preparation

- Set up stations around the table for each step with signs for each topic and the materials that they will need to create an item for their platter.

- Write questions for the "Feelings Matter" exercise on newsprint; attach them to the walls in an arrangement that allows participants to move freely from station to station.

- Put tradition statements from the "Who Belongs at the Margin? Who Belongs at the Center?" exercise (page 107) on color-coded (one color for each statement) note cards. Prepare enough sets of six statements for each member of the group to receive a set. If available, set up another room for this exercise by marking off sections identified as the center, margins, and rejected.

Question Prayer (page 95)

Invite each member of the group to write down one question that she or he has for God about what it means to participate in this group. Encourage members of the group to get started with the sentence completions that are included in the text.

If the group has a difficult time understanding what it means to ask God questions, allow someone to share a moment in their lives when they sought guidance through prayer by asking God a question. Reassure them that there is no such thing as a "stupid question."

If members of the group feel embarrassed about asking God about issues related to sexuality, ask them to describe, as honestly as they can, what feels uncomfortable about talking to God about sexuality. Some may feel that talking about sex is "dirty" or that sex is behavior that seeks selfish pleasure, and while it is okay to apologize to God for sexual sins, we cannot specifically and openly "talk" to God about sexuality. After naming the concerns, inhibitions, and discomfort of the group, invite the group to pray:

> Precious God, can we talk to you about our feelings of . . . [read the list that the group has generated]? Is it okay to talk to you about sexuality? With humility, sincerity, and openness, we lift up these feelings and questions to you. In the name of Jesus Christ we pray. Amen.

Exercise 1: Make a Tradition Platter (page 96)

This exercise includes family food traditions, spoken traditions about sexuality, and unspoken traditions about sexuality. Permit participants to sit quietly while they reflect on their memories. It may help for them to go to a station: brainstorm four or five ideas, then select one or two of those ideas to put on the platter.

Remember that family memories can bring up sentimental, fond moments of happiness as well as painful and disturbing moments of rejection and isolation. Participants do not have to share anything that makes them uncomfortable or upset.

For recollections about family food traditions, prompt the members of your group by asking them to think about any traditions that they have been taught or have observed that are related to holidays, family celebrations, styles of cooking, or recipes for food. Identify traditions that they value as well as traditions that they may not particularly like.

Spoken traditions about sexuality and unspoken traditions about sexuality may be sensitive areas for people to recall. If they are not comfortable discussing family traditions, they may try recalling what was spoken and unspoken about sexuality at school or in television sitcoms about family life that they watched as children.

Exercise 2: "Who Said What?" Skit (page 98)

Assign the parts of the play to members of your group to read aloud. The Tour Guide and the Questioner are the biggest parts, so assign these to your most eager group participants. Have fun with it!

Exercise 3: Feelings Matter (page 106)

This is an opportunity to debrief the information that was in the "Who Said What?" skit. Focus first on what was heard and then on their opinions about it. Make sure that the incomplete sentences have already been written down on sheets of newsprint with one sentence per sheet and attached to the walls.

Exercise 4: Who Belongs at the Margin? Who Belongs at the Center? (page 107)

1. Using three chairs, designate the middle of the room, the edge of the room, and the space just outside the room or in the doorway.

2. Remind the group that these designated areas are for *their* own understandings of what should be central, marginal, and rejected aspects of Christian tradition.

3. Hand each member of your group a set of the six statements.

4. Read the statements one at a time, allowing the members of the group to decide where to place the statement, e.g., in the center, marginal, or rejected area.

5. Allow the group about five minutes to reflect on the choices that have been made by others in the group besides themselves. This is a chance to think about tradition as something that is more than an individual matter of acceptance or rejection. It's also a chance to notice whose views are missing from your group and to consider what difference that makes. If your group tends to be quite similar in its choices, they should consider what it means to include perspectives that are not represented in the room.

6. Identifying the criteria used to designate statements as central, marginal, or rejected allows participants to articulate why the next generation needs these traditions. They should think of themselves as passing down traditions that will enable their own children, nieces, nephews, or the children in their Sunday school program to develop healthy understandings of spirituality and sexuality. Prompt members to describe their criteria beginning with: "What matters to me is that they know..."

Journaling

Invite the participants to think about some of the changes in their own sexual journey and the ways that Christian faith has been available to help them as those changes have taken place.

Closing Prayer (page 110)

In the closing prayer we celebrate the "great cloud of witnesses" that have gone before us. The names lifted up can be people the participants have known personally as well as well-known leaders.

FACILITATOR'S GUIDE TO SESSION SIX: Building Good Community, Keeping Faith

Materials Needed

- Paper, crayons, pens, and pencils
- Newsprint and markers or presentation software to record the ideas of your group
- Large bowl with candles, sand, matches

Preparation

Prepare the large bowl for the "Ritual of Gratitude." Fill the bowl with sand and put unlit candles in the sand. Bury the base of the candles far enough so they are stable and safe when lit. You need matches and enough candles for each person in your group. Find the words for the hymn "Spirit of the Living God" in case people need them.

Body Prayer (page 115)

Invite the participants to relax and be playful as they follow the directions for this prayer. Be mindful that some members may not be as physically flexible as others, so have fun trying to follow all of the directions, but adjustments are fine. Also make adjustments for the

size of your group. Afterward, you may want to briefly discuss how
it felt to do this prayer. What felt uncomfortable or comfortable and
why? How did it resemble what it means to be part of the church?

Exercise 1: "All Four of Them Come to Visit!" (page 116)

This could be a challenging exercise for the group, so keep track of
the responses that are needed. Brainstorm some ideas before the
session so you can prompt the participants if they need help. Before
taking turns going into the center, spend a brief time in the four corners thinking about what is the role of the assigned resource. How
does it independently contribute to the task of doing theology? Encourage corner participants to think about how the center resource
tests, validates, or contributes knowledge for the work they must do.

After they've worked so hard using one side of their brain to articulate connections between these resources, invite them to use the
other side of their brain to creatively illustrate those connections.
Provide crayons, pencils, and paper so they can draw diagrams or
pictures. Encourage them to draw any kind of symbolic representa-
tion of the relationship between the four resources of faith, using
images that range from wild, swirling constructions or overlapping
colors or to familiar, symmetrical shapes.

Exercise 2: Learning from David's Story (page 118)

Decide the best way to read the story aloud to your group: one
person could read the whole story instead of assigning parts.

Welcome conversations that arise about why and how they may
feel unable to imagine themselves in the same situation as David.

Since this story takes place in an African American church,
depending upon the makeup of your group, some may not be immediately able to place themselves in this situation. Encourage them
to *try* to imagine themselves in this church funeral setting. If they are
concerned about racial/ethnic differences between their own background and David's, encourage them to describe what they believe
those differences to be. Ask them to explain how those cultural differences would shape the way that they employ experience, scripture,
tradition, and reason.

In addition, some may find it difficult to imagine themselves as a gay male who has lost a beloved friend. Encourage them to talk about any discomfort. Allow them to describe how those differences matter, especially how sexual orientation shapes their theology.

Exercise 3: A Christian Conferencing Fishbowl (page 122)

A fishbowl activity involves risk taking. Remind participants to allow each character to express herself or himself. Tell the chairperson to have at least one prayer and one silent time. When deciding when to stop the role-play, don't worry about whether the group has made a final decision on who to hire. The purpose is to practice the process of Christian Conferencing.

Immediately after the role-play ends, keep the group focused on feelings, not explanations or criticisms of the role-play. All participants could start off by offering one word to describe their emotional response.

For Step Three: review the statement about making comparisons between race/ethnicity and sexuality that is found in the introduction of this book (see pages 20–21).

Evaluation

Remember that evaluation is important for the group. Each member's opinion is valuable. Their responses do not need to be shared with the entire group, but if your group would like to openly evaluate the study, encourage them to express their appreciation as well as disappointments. Also remind them to use "I" language. Instead of "this study was too..." say, "I found this study to be...," or "I wish that we could have..."

> Covenant — This exercise should be completed individually in the way each person feels most comfortable.
>
> Ritual — This is an opportunity to make sure that each member of the group feels appreciated and supported.

Closing Prayer (page 128)

This prayer can be read aloud in unison.

Glossary

Canon. The scriptures approved by official councils of the ancient church that came to be considered holy and authoritative for Christian churches, and included in the Bible.

C.E. Common Era, also referred to in some Christian circles as A.D., after the death and resurrection of Jesus Christ, and designates the era of human history Christians share in common with people of all religious faiths and cultural backgrounds.

Christian Conferencing. A process of discernment for group decision making by Christians that involves prayer and dialogue (not debate) with one another to determine God's will for the church.

Coming Out. The process a person undergoes as he or she discovers, accepts, integrates, and lives out his or her sexual orientation or transgender identity.

Cruising. From the verb "to cruise." An activity that some individuals engage in to solicit anonymous sexual encounters with other individuals.

Embodiment Theology. A theology that affirms human bodies as blessed by God rather than inherently evil or sinful and stresses the incarnation of God in Jesus Christ.

Gender. A socially constructed category that assigns particular labels to human physical attributes and characteristics, such as labeling bodies with vaginas as female, or facial whiskers and beards as male.

Genitalization. The reduction of sexuality to sexual acts, and of sexual acts to genital expression.

Gospel. The good tidings of the realm of God brought by Jesus the Christ characterized by the central teachings of love of God and love of neighbor.

Heterosexism. The system of advantages bestowed on heterosexuals granting them superior status and rights in the culture and institutions of society only because of their sexual orientation as heterosexuals.

Heterosexual Ally. A heterosexual person who supports and honors diversity in sex/gender identities as well as sexual orientation, and who acts accordingly to interrupt and challenge homophobic and heterosexist remarks and actions of others, and who is willing to explore these forms of bias within himself or herself.

Homophobia. The fear and hatred of same-sex sexual behavior and attraction.

Incarnation. God coming into our midst in the person of Jesus of Nazareth. The humanity of God implies that our embodied existence and our sexuality are integral to who we are and how we express our love with others.

Intersex. Persons whose anatomical makeup at birth includes a combination of sexual organs, chromosomes, and physical features that are usually not found in one person, and which make the conventional assignment of a single sex/gender impossible. The majority of intersexed people are surgically assigned a gender at birth. Replaces the term "hermaphrodite," which is now considered misleading.

Intimacy. Physical, emotional, and spiritual closeness with another person.

Job's Daughters. A Masonic organization for girls and young women.

LGBT. Commonly stands for Lesbian, Gay, Bisexual, Transgender communities. Although "GLBT" is sometimes used, we have purposely listed Lesbian first to subvert the traditional power structure of males as most important. Elsewhere, there may be a "Q" added to acknowledge those who have questions about their sexual orientation and/or sex/gender identity and do not want to be identified in any particular category. "Q" also refers to "Queer" and is a way of claiming a term historically used by heterosexuals to express hatred and derision to instead express pride in unique, minority sexual identities and cultural expression (e.g., Queer theory). "Q" is also often meant to serve as an umbrella term. There may also be an "I" for those who are Intersexed.

Our Whole Lives (OWL). A series of sexuality education curricula for different age groups. OWL helps participants make informed and responsible decisions about their sexual health and behavior by equipping them with accurate, age-appropriate information in sex subject areas. See www.uua.org/owl.

Pedophilia. The act or fantasy on the part of an adult of engaging in sexual activity with a child or children; sexual perversion in which children are the preferred sexual object. While the myth persists that gay men are child molesters and recruit children into their "lifestyle," the facts reveal that the majority of child molesters are heterosexual men.

Racial/ethnic. A socially constructed identity that categorizes persons according to a combination of factors related to one's outward physical appearance; social history, such as country of origin of self and family members/ancestors; language and habits; and the cultural system of granting status and privileges in one's society.

Sensuality. The human capacity for enjoyment of one's own, as well as another's, physical body and presence.

Sex. As a noun, it is rooted in some biological trait. However, studies of physical characteristics and chromosomes require a more fluid designation than our traditional two distinctions of male and female allow. Some persons are born with combinations of genitalia, body parts, and chromosomes that do not easily fit into traditional categories of male or female (see Intersex).

Sex/Gender Identity. A socially constructed category that assigns particular labels to traits related to both sexuality (physical aspects) as well as gender (social roles).

Sexual identity. The development (often lifelong) of an awareness of one's wants, needs, and desires related to sexuality, often linked to gender roles and traits.

Sexuality. Human characteristics related to physical makeup such as hormones and genitals, emotional and spiritual expression, and formation of intimate bonds with other human beings.

Sexualization. The use of sexuality to influence, control, and manipulate others. Examples include rape, incest, sexual harassment, seduction, and flirting.

Transgender(ed). An umbrella term used to describe persons who cross gender boundaries. It includes transsexuals, gender benders, cross dressers, and those born with ambiguous sexual characteristics (see Intersex).

Transsexuals. Persons whose outward physical attributes do not match their inner gender identity. Includes postoperative persons and those for whom sexual reassignment surgery is not planned (nonoperative transsexual).

Welcoming Movement. Campaign in various Protestant denominations to fully welcome LGBT persons into the life of the church. Some of these organizations advocate the end of the church's institutional discrimination in the areas of ordination, marriage, membership, etc. Official national organizations include: Affirming (United Church of Canada), More Light Presbyterians, Integrity (Episcopal), Open and Affirming (United Church of Christ and Disciples of Christ), Reconciling in Christ (Lutheran), Reconciling Ministries Network (United Methodists), Welcoming and Affirming (American Baptist), Welcoming (Unitarian

Universalist). Some denominations, including the Metropolitan Community Church (MCC) and Unity Fellowship, originated with a ministry to LGBT. There are pro-LGBT communities beyond Protestant traditions, including Dignity (Catholic), The World Congress of GLBT Jews, and Affirmation: Gay and Lesbian Mormons.

White Privilege. Rights, advantages, benefits, or immunity granted to white persons (usually those of European descent) identifying them as norm, center, and superior in U.S. culture.

Notes

Introduction

1. Revon Kyle Banneker interview with Rev. Carl Bean in *Sojourner: Black Gay Voices in the Age of AIDS*, vol. 2, ed. B. Michael Hunter (New York: Other Countries, 1993).

2. www.apa/org/pubinfo/answers.html.

3. Ibid.

4. www.pcusa.org/101/101-homosexual.htm. A study of human sexuality encouraging dialogue is entitled "Presbyterians and Human Sexuality 1991," Publication #OGA-91-001.

5. www.religioustolerance.org.

6. Ibid.

7. Ibid.

8. www.mcchurch.org.

9. www.united-church.ca/jpc/humanrights/030516.shtm.

10. "Human Sexuality and the Christian Faith" [a study] (ELCA Division of Church in Society, 1991), 33.

11. Sixty-eighth General Convention Resolution #1985-DO82, *Journal of the General Convention of The Episcopal Church, Anaheim, 1985* (New York: General Convention, 1986), 207.

12. www.abc-usa.org.

13. Richard Hooker (1554–1600) was a foundational theologian for the Anglican tradition. "It is widely recognized that it was Hooker who first advanced within the post-Reformation English Church the use of reason as an essential ingredient in order to act as a counterpoise to Calvin's appeal to Scripture and Rome's appeal to tradition." *Nigel Atkinson, Richard Hooker and the Authority of Scripture, Tradition and Reason* (Carlisle, Cumbria, UK: Paternoster Press, 1997), 1. In the late twentieth century, Methodist Albert Outler reinforced the four resources as critical for the Methodist theological task. Catholics add revelation to

the mix. For Catholicism, the relationship between tradition, scripture, and revelation is described in G. F. Van Ackeren, "Theology," *New Catholic Encyclopedia*, 2nd ed. (Detroit: Thomson Gale, 2003).

14. Renee L. Hill, *A Whosoever Church: Welcoming Lesbians and Gay Men into African American Congregations*, ed. Gary David Comstock (Louisville: Westminster John Knox Press, 2001), 197.

15. www.moss-fritch.com/Rev_Swenson.html.

Session One: Can We Talk?

16. Miroslav Volf, *Exclusion and Embrace: A Theological Exploration of Identity, Otherness, and Reconciliation* (Nashville: Abingdon Press, 1996), 20.

17. www.religioustolerance.org/hom_disc.html.

18. Ibid.

19. Jack M. Tuell, "How I Changed My Mind," sermon preached at Claremont United Methodist Church, Claremont, California, May 18, 2003.

20. *Our Whole Lives* (OWL), a series of sexuality education curricula, is the result of seven years of collaborative effort by the Unitarian Universalist Association and the United Church of Christ's Board for Homeland Ministries, 25 (www.uua.org/owl).

21. Kelly Brown Douglas, *Sexuality and the Black Church: A Womanist Perspective* (Maryknoll, N.Y.: Orbis Books, 1999), 115.

22. James B. Nelson, *Body Theology* (Louisville: Westminster/John Knox Press, 1992), 22.

23. "Presbyterians and Human Sexuality Study 1991," publication no. OGA-91-001, 8. (It can be ordered for $5.00 + S&H by phoning 800-524-2612.)

24. "Sexuality: Some Common Convictions," adopted by the Church Council of the Evangelical Lutheran Church, November 9, 1996.

25. *The United Methodist Book of Discipline* (Nashville: United Methodist Publishing, 1984).

26. James B. Nelson, *The Intimate Connection: Male Sexuality and Masculine Spirituality* (Philadelphia: Westminster Press, 1988).

27. Jay, interview conducted by Karen Oliveto, July 3, 2003.

Session Two: Are We Theologians?

28. www.maxpages.com/louicia/The_Lord_is_my_Programmer.

29. www.io.com/~rga/saying248.html.

30. Carlos L. Dews and Carolyn Leste Law, eds., *Out in the South* (Philadelphia: Temple University Press, 2001), 47.

31. www.united-church.ca/news/2003/0620.shtm.

Session Three: Experience

32. Interview conducted by Karen Oliveto, May 22, 2002.

33. Clair, interview conducted by Karen Oliveto, July 8, 2003.

Session Four: Scripture

34. Mark Jordan, *The Invention of Sodomy in Christian Theology* (Chicago: University of Chicago Press, 1997), 30.

35. Peter Gomes, *The Good Book: Reading the Bible with Mind and Heart* (New York: William Morrow and Company, 1996), 152.

Session Five: Sex and Tradition

36. Loraine Hutchins and Lani Kaahumanu, eds., *Bi Any Other Name: Bisexual People Speak Out* (Boston: Alyson Publications, 1991), 202.

37. Dews and Law, *Out in the South*, 97–98.

38. Kevin K. Kumashiro, ed. *Troubling Intersections of Race and Sexuality: Queer Students of Color and Anti-Oppressive Education* (Lanham, Md.: Rowman & Littlefield, 2001), 131.

39. Merry E. Wiesner-Hanks, *Regulating Desire, Reforming Practice* (New York: Routledge, 2000), 170–71.

40. Kumashiro, *Troubling Intersections of Race and Sexuality*, 155.

41. Augustine, *The Trinity*, ed. Edmund Hill, O.P. (Brooklyn, N.Y.: New City Press, 1991), Book 12, chap. 3, 328.

42. Augustine, *The City of God*, trans. Henry Bettenson (London: Penguin Books), Book 14, chap. 16, 577.

43. Augustine, "The Good of Marriage," in *Fathers of the Church: Treatises on Marriage and Other Subjects*, vol. 27 (New York: Fathers of the Church, Inc., 1955), Book 8, chap. 8, 20.

44. Thomas Aquinas, *Summa Theologica*, ed. and trans. Edmund Hill (London: Blackfriars, 1964), Part I, Question 92, Article 1, 37–39.

45. Julian of Norwich, *The Book of Showings to the Anchoress Julian of Norwich*, trans. James Walsh (New York: Harper and Row, 1979), chaps. 58, 59, 159–61; quoted in Rosemary Radford Ruether's *Women and Redemption: A Theological History* (Minneapolis: Fortress Press, 1998), 110.

46. Ibid., 110–11.

47. Hildegard of Bingen, *Scivias*, trans. Mother Columba Hart and Jane Bishop (Mahwah, N.J.: Paulist Press: 1990), Book II, Vision 6, Chapter 76, 278.

48. Ibid., Book II, Vision 6, Chapter 78, 279.

49. Ibid.

50. Ibid.

51. From an Italian manuscript of the early Middle Ages, quoted in John Boswell, "Homosexuality and Religious Life: A Historical Approach," in *Sexuality and the Sacred: Sources for Theological Reflection*, ed. James B. Nelson and Sandra P. Longfellow (Louisville: Westminster John Knox Press, 1994), 368.

52. Martin Luther, *Lectures on Genesis*, chapters 1–5 in *Luther's Works*, vol. 1, ed. Jaroslav Pelikan (St. Louis: Concordia Publishing House, 1958), 115.

53. Martin Luther, "The Estate of Marriage," in *Luther's Works: The Christian in Society*, vol. 45, ed. Walter I. Brandt (Philadelphia: Muhlenberg Press, 1962), Part II, 31–32.

54. Ibid., 32.

55. John Calvin, *The Institutes of the Christian Religion*, vol. 1, ed. John T. McNeill (Philadelphia: Westminster Press, 1960), 407.

56. John Wesley, "Thoughts on a Single Life" [1765] in *Works of John Wesley* (London: Wesleyan Methodist Reading Room, 1872; repr. Peabody, Mass.: Hendrickson, 1894), no. 15, 463.

57. Henry Abelove, *The Evangelist of Desire: John Wesley and the Methodists* (Stanford, Calif.: Stanford University Press, 1990), 53.

58. Presbyterian Church (USA).

59. Erin K. Swenson, address to the Presbytery of San Francisco, January 14, 2003.

Session Six: Building Good Community, Keeping Faith

60. Beulah, interview conducted by Karen Oliveto, May 15, 2003.

61. Keith Boykin, *One More River to Cross: Black and Gay in America* (New York: Doubleday, 1996), 123–24.

Facilitator's Guide

62. Adapted from Tracy E. Ore, "A Guided Fantasy," in *The Sociology of Sexuality and Sexual Orientation: Syllabi and Teaching Materials*, ed. Tracy E. Ore, 4th ed. (Washington, D.C.: American Sociological Association, 2002), 197.